DECONSTRUCTION

DECONSTRUCTION

DAVID J. GUNKEL

The MIT Press | Cambridge, Massachusetts | London, England

This book was set in Chaparral Pro by New Best-set Typesetters Ltd. Printed and bound in the United States of America.

Library of Congress Cataloging-in-Publication Data

Names: Gunkel, David J., author.
Title: Deconstruction / David J. Gunkel.
Description: Cambridge, Massachusetts ; London, England : The MIT Press, 2021. | Series: The MIT Press essential knowledge series | Includes bibliographical references and index.
Identifiers: LCCN 2020031703 | ISBN 9780262542470 (paperback)
Subjects: LCSH: Deconstruction.
Classification: LCC B809.6 .G865 2021 | DDC 149/.97—dc23
LC record available at https://lccn.loc.gov/2020031703

10   9   8   7   6   5   4   3   2   1

In memory of my friend and colleague Ciro Marcondes Filho

CONTENTS

SERIES FOREWORD

The MIT Press Essential Knowledge series offers accessible, concise, beautifully produced pocket-size books on topics of current interest. Written by leading thinkers, the books in this series deliver expert overviews of subjects that range from the cultural and the historical to the scientific and the technical.

In today's era of instant information gratification, we have ready access to opinions, rationalizations, and superficial descriptions. Much harder to come by is the foundational knowledge that informs a principled understanding of the world. Essential Knowledge books fill that need. Synthesizing specialized subject matter for nonspecialists and engaging critical topics through fundamentals, each of these compact volumes offers readers a point of access to complex ideas.

PREFACE

I have been involved with deconstruction from the beginning of my professional career. I came of age, academically speaking, at the end of the twentieth century. During that time deconstruction was the *cause célèbre* in a variety of academic fields and disciplines, and I had the unique opportunity to study and work with a number of the leading innovators in philosophy and deconstruction: John Sallis at Loyola University in Chicago and David Farrell Krell and Michael Naas at DePaul University. I also had the good fortune to have met and talked with Jacques Derrida on two occasions. The first was at a conference that John Sallis had organized to commemorate the hundredth anniversary of the birth of Martin Heidegger. The event was held at Loyola University in Chicago, September 21–24, 1989. The second took place during the colloquium "*Das Unheimliche*: Philosophy, Architecture, The City," which was organized by David Farrell Krell at DePaul University, April 26–27, 1991.

My own research efforts have sought to develop the equivalent of an academic API (application programming interface) between deconstruction and the philosophy of technology. This work began by way of an engagement with architecture and collaborations with one of the architects involved in the DePaul University colloquium: Ben

Nicholson, who was, at that time, attached to the Illinois Institute of Technology. These interactions resulted in a number of publications, museum exhibits, and a documentary film about the B-52 bomber, produced and directed by Hartmut Bitomsky.

Shortly thereafter, I began connecting the dots between the techniques of deconstruction and information and communication technology (ICT), using what I had learned from Derrida and others to facilitate deconstruction of the Internet, virtual worlds, digital computers, and artificial intelligence. But there was, as I discovered, one persistent obstacle to the success of this endeavor. Few individuals outside the very small community of academic philosophers with whom I had been associated knew what deconstruction was, or worse, had a mistaken understanding of what they thought it must be from the numerous misrepresentations that had been (for better or worse) easily available in both the academic and popular media. In an effort to address this problem, I included in my first book—*Hacking Cyberspace* (2001)—an appendix with the rather ham-fisted title "Deconstruction for Dummies." And in every book since that first publication, I have found it necessary to update, rework, and/or reiterate that basic explanation in one way or another.

This book is the product of what is now a quarter century of effort to make sense of deconstruction and to make it make sense in a way that can directly address the opportunities and challenges of the twenty-first century. It leverages the successes and frustrations of these previous explainers and provides a presentation of the material that is accessible, concise, and easy to use. Like all the EKS titles, *Deconstruction* has been deliberately designed to get readers up to speed quickly and efficiently, providing both novice and pro with a compact and accessible version of the fundamentals. What is called "deconstruction" has had the unfortunate reputation for being heady intellectual stuff for ivory-tower navel-gazers. This book is designed to deconstruct that, and bring it all down to earth.

The specific approach to the material that is presented here has benefited from decades of interactions and conversations with individuals and communities who have made a real difference in my own life and work. I cannot possibly name them all. But there is one individual who needs to be explicitly identified, my wife Ann Hetzel Gunkel, who has been my constant companion and sounding board for all of these things since before graduate school. This book would not have been possible without her love, support, and incredible insights into all things academic and otherwise.

Finally, the writing took place and had its place during the period of self-isolation that was imposed on the world in response to the COVID-19 pandemic in the early months of the year 2020. In the numbered sequence of titles bearing my name, this is my thirteenth book, which some might interpret as an unlucky number. And at times it seemed—in the face of the uncertainties and incomplete information regarding the virus and its impact—that it might be accompanied by misfortune. At this point—at the time of the writing of this preface—all of this remains undecidable. But that's life. And, as we shall soon see in the pages that follow, that's also deconstruction.

INTRODUCTION

Deconstruction, the word at least, is familiar, perhaps too familiar. We rush to purchase the newest deconstructed jackets and slouchy bags from designer labels to wear to events in newly rehabilitated historic buildings that have a deconstructivist architectural aesthetic where we enjoy deconstructed salads while debating the fine points of the current administration's plan to deconstruct one or another aspect of the bloated welfare state. Despite this seemingly unrestrained proliferation of the word across the vernacular, "deconstruction" remains a kind of slippery signifier and empty placeholder. We all kind of know or at least think we have a sense of what the word indicates. And yet, if you ask someone to explain it, what you typically get is a rather confused shell game of word substitutions, where "deconstruction" is loosely associated with other concepts like "disassembly," "destruction," "reverse engineering," or "the act of taking something apart."[1]

Despite the circulation of these familiar (mis)understandings, the term "deconstruction" does not indicate something negative. What it signifies is neither simply synonymous with destruction nor the opposite of construction. As Jacques Derrida, the fabricator of the neologism and progenitor of the concept, pointed out in the afterword to the book *Limited Inc*: "The 'de-' of deconstruction signifies not the demolition of what is constructing itself, but rather what remains to be thought beyond the constructionist or destructionist schema."[2] For this reason, deconstruction is something entirely other than what is typically understood and delimited by the conceptual opposition situated between the two terms "construction" and "destruction." In fact, to put it schematically, deconstruction comprises a kind of general strategy by which to intervene in this and all the other logical oppositions and conceptual dichotomies that have and continue to organize how we think and how we speak.

But quoting and referring to the authority of Derrida does not necessarily clarify things. In addition to being credited as the "father of deconstruction"[3] (something that will be thoroughly questioned and evaluated in what follows), the one thing most people know about Derrida, or at least have heard about Derrida, is that he writes things that are notoriously difficult, if not impossible to

"The 'de-' of deconstruc-
tion signifies not the
demolition of what is
constructing itself, but
rather what remains to
be thought beyond the
constructionist or
destructionist schema."

read. This reputation for being unreadable is widespread and seemingly inescapable. Consider, for example, the following comment from Christopher Orlet's obituary of Derrida, which was published in *The American Spectator* on October 15, 2004: "If Derrida's works are not widely read it is because of a ponderous style that makes them all but unreadable.... After only one round of Derrida one heads back to the corner on wobbly legs, badly shaken, ready to throw in the towel. What in God's name is the man getting at, and why on Earth doesn't he just say it and have done with it?"[4]

Summarily dismissing Derrida and his publications as unreadable is a sure-fire way to not understand anything at all about deconstruction. But we should also not kid ourselves or pretend. Reading Derrida is difficult—at times exceedingly difficult—but doing so is an investment that will pay off and be well worth the effort. To put it another way, Derrida's writing does not immediately yield to the efforts of reading. The text seems to be deliberately designed to resist its reader. Although this might sound like a stupid move, or at least an unfortunate oversight, on the part of an author who wishes to communicate some content to his audience, there are good reasons for this. Namely, it puts in question and problematizes the unquestioned assumptions of reading and meaning making that are all too often taken for granted and not explicitly made the target of critical inquiry and reflection. Reading a work on deconstruction, therefore, also involves and must necessarily be a deconstruction of reading.

This book sorts out the terminology, the concept, and the practices of deconstruction. It does so not simply to correct misunderstandings and misuses of the word, but also to provide students, researchers, educators, activists, and curious-minded individuals with a powerful conceptual tool kit for thinking and acting differently in the world. Because deconstruction identifies a kind of general strategy for challenging existing conceptual structures and "thinking outside the box" of existing logical formations, it equips individuals with a kind of super power for engaging with and rethinking all aspects of contemporary life—from questions concerning personal identity to the exigencies of environmental degradation and global climate change, from debates across the political spectrum to the opportunities and challenges of new and emerging technological systems. The objective of the book, therefore, is to provide readers with the essential knowledge necessary to understand what deconstruction is, what it can be useful for, and how one goes about mobilizing it in a variety of different fields, disciplines, and contexts.

The presentation is divided into four chapters. We begin in chapter 2 by "going negative." That is, we start the investigation by defining what deconstruction is not or should not be confused with. Beginning in this way is standard operating procedure (SOP), insofar as we often define something that is unknown by differentiating it from things that are already known and more familiar. But a negative definition, though necessary for getting things started, is never sufficient in and of itself. For that reason, chapters 3 and 4 provide for a more substantive formulation. Chapter 3 develops an abstract and schematic characterization that is derived from Derrida's own efforts to reflect on the procedures, protocols, and processes of deconstruction. This schematic diagram is actualized in chapter 4 by examining four examples or instances where deconstruction has a place or has taken place. Providing both an abstract schematic followed by specific instances and examples once again is SOP for this kind of effort. But it also mobilizes a set of conceptual differences (i.e., abstract/particular, general/specific) that deconstruction deconstructs. Therefore, from the beginning we will need to pay attention to this performative recoil, whereby what comes to be said about deconstruction is already implicated in and complicated by deconstruction. Finally, chapter 5 will conclude with a cost-benefit analysis. There are many things deconstruction is good for and can do for us, but it also has costs that need to be explicitly identified and reckoned with. Like a new wonder drug, deconstruction has its effects, and it has its side effects. Chapter 5 provides a detailed consideration of both.

GOING NEGATIVE

Providing a definition of "deconstruction" is difficult, if not endlessly frustrating. For this reason, this chapter is going to be overwhelmingly negative, mobilizing statements that seek to articulate what deconstruction is not, or should not be mistaken as being. Beginning in this way has both advantages and disadvantages. On the one hand, the definition of something—a word, a technical term, a concept—often gets underway by indicating what it is not and drawing distinctions between it and other things that are different from it. On the other hand, trying to define or otherwise characterize something by describing what it isn't is not only unsatisfying—like playing a game of twenty questions, where every answer is "no"—but also of little substance or consequence. If I tell you "deconstruction is not a color" that statement, although entirely correct, provides very little by way of actual content.

Interestingly and especially for our purposes this tension between (1) the discursive exigencies of negative definition (i.e., telling someone what something is by first informing them what it is not) and (2) the fact that such characterizations are rather empty and provide very little by way of usable information, is itself the kind of logical problem that deconstruction is specifically formulated to address and resolve. Consequently, to begin by going negative is both unavoidable and (at the same time) not without its own complications. But doing so already tells us something—or, perhaps better stated, *shows* us something—about deconstruction that could not otherwise be explicitly formulated or described. It is, in other words, a necessary but not sufficient first step.

Derrida Is Not the "Father of Deconstruction"

The word "deconstruction" is commonly associated with the work of French philosopher Jacques Derrida (1930–2004), who has often been called "the father of deconstruction." Deconstruction, however, resists this paternal identification. The word—already in the beginning and at its point of origination—exceeds the decisive actions, knowledge, and/or control of its supposed progenitor. Instead, "deconstruction" emerges at a particular moment and imposes itself on the one who is then retroactively miscredited with having developed and introduced the term.

Derrida tried to provide an account of this—in effect, responding for the fact that he himself could not take paternal responsibility for the word—in a short text that was originally written to help guide efforts to translate "deconstruction" into Japanese. "When I choose this word," Derrida explains, "or when it imposed itself on me—I think it was in *Of Grammatology*—I little thought it would be credited with such a central role in the discourse that interested me at the time. Among other things I wished to translate and adapt to my own ends the Heideggerian word *Destruktion*."[1]

What is noteworthy about this statement is that Derrida does not take credit for inventing, devising, or introducing either the word or the concept of deconstruction. He does not write, for instance, "When I coined or introduced the word 'deconstruction,'" or "When I decided or determined to call this 'deconstruction,'" or some other statement that would attribute the coming-into-being of the word and practice to some individual effort or deliberate action. There is, instead, a kind of original passivity. Although Derrida initially writes "when I choose this word," he immediately revises the statement, reversing the direction of the action and proper attribution: "when it imposed itself on me." Deconstruction, therefore, does not conform to the usual model of agency, authorial intention, and paternal authority. With deconstruction, it is the word that imposes itself on its author.

This characterization is consistent with a questioning of authority and reformulation of the author function that had been developed in the work of twentieth-century theorists like Roland Barthes and Michel Foucault (the latter was, since we are taking about paternal relationships, one of Derrida's teachers). The figure of the author is not some eternal Platonic form but comprises a social construct that comes into existence at a particular time, for a particular purpose, and in service to a particular set of interests. And if this figure has a beginning, a point in time when it is initially deployed and authorized to occupy this place of authority, it also has an end, a point at which this configuration is no longer operative or useful. As Foucault explained: "Although, since the eighteenth century, the author has played the role of the regulator of the fictive . . . it does not seem necessary that the author function remain constant in form, complexity, and even in existence. I think that, as our society changes, at the very moment when it is in the process of changing, the author function will disappear."[2] It is this disappearance and withdrawal of what had been the principal figure of literary authority that is announced and marked by the title to Barthes's seemingly apocalyptic essay "Death of the Author."[3] What this phrase indicates is not the end of life of any particular individual, but rather the termination and closure of the figure of the author as the ultimate authority over the text and the kind of textual criticism that had been organized around the "man and his works" model.

Deconstruction solicits, leverages, and extends this questioning of the assumed authority that had been granted to the author over his (or her) work. The parenthetical in this sentence is of crucial importance. It points to the fact that, at least since the time of Plato's *Phaedrus*, the author—the principal figure of authority in matters regarding all forms of textual production—had been defined and characterized as a father (therefore gendered male) and that this "fact" needs to be subjected to and has been the subject of deconstruction. This challenge to the legacy and logic of what Derrida called "phallogocentrism" has been especially influential for and important to postcolonial feminist theorists, artists, and writers, like Trinh T. Minh-ha, Gayatri Chakravorty Spivak, and Donna Haraway. For our purposes (for the effort to define and characterize deconstruction), this deconstruction of authority has least three important consequences:

1. It is the main reason why—despite the fact that we have (here and now) already been calling upon and deploying "Derrida" as a kind of authority figure— one cannot and should not appeal to the authority of this particular author as the final word on the proper meaning and use of the word "deconstruction." The

person presumed to be the go-to expert and final authority, namely Derrida, has already problematized and withdrawn the very rhetorical gesture of making an appeal to authority, such as saying anything authoritative in the name of Derrida.

2. Following from this, it can be said—and it must be emphasized—that Derrida is not the progenitor or the "father of deconstruction." He is, and he understood and explained himself to be, just another reader of and respondent to the occurrences or events of deconstruction that have always and already been at work and therefore operating in excess of the authority of any one author. Recognizing this, however, does raise important political and ethical questions. These questions haunted Derrida throughout his career, and they continue to be an important matter for debate.[4]

3. At the same time, this dispersion of authority and dissemination of responsibility also open the space for what will later be criticized, by Derrida and many others, as the domestication or commodification of deconstruction in various fields and endeavors but especially within literary criticism in the United States. Because Derrida had already and quite strategically abdicated the authorial throne and relinquished paternal authority over the term "deconstruction," anyone and

everyone can and has (mis)appropriated[5] it to name all kinds of different things. This will turn out to be (as we shall soon see) both a blessing and a curse.

Deconstruction Is Not Negative

The term "deconstruction" emerges or imposes itself (and the passive construction is quite deliberate) in the course of an effort to translate and adapt the Heideggerian word *Destruktion*.[6] This word appears in Martin Heidegger's 1927 magnum opus, *Being and Time*, to identify what was supposed to have been the second main part of the book. The first part—the part actually written and published— was designed to analyze the meaning of Being by way of an interpretation of human existence or *Dasein*. The second part, which was not published as planned but only proposed, was to be what Heidegger called "a phenomenological *destruktion* of the history of ontology."[7] Despite initial appearances this was not (not for Heidegger, at least) a negative undertaking, such as the demolition of the history of ontology or a simple leveling of the tradition. It was intended to have a positive trajectory and outcome. For Heidegger, *Destruktion* was supposed to unearth or retrieve from the sediment of the history of philosophy the "forgetting of the question of Being" that had been the defining condition of Western thought.

Following from this effort to translate and adapt the Heideggerian word *destruktion*, it also can be said that "deconstruction" is not negative. The word does not indicate "to take apart," "to un-construct," or "to disassemble." Despite this widespread and rather popular misconception, which has become something of an institutional (mal) practice, deconstruction is neither a form of destructive analysis or criticism, nor a kind of demolition or dismantlement, nor the process of reverse engineering. As Derrida emphasizes in the course of a radio interview from 1986 (and you can almost hear the exasperated frustration in his voice): "Deconstruction, let's say it one more time, is not demolition or destruction."[8] If deconstruction were a destruction, then it would be hard to escape the conclusion that what it names would be a form of nihilism, where "nothing would be possible any longer."[9] But that is explicitly and definitely not the case.

However, to declare that deconstruction is not negative does not mean (by way of the grammatical/logical form of the double negative) that it is something positive, like a mode of construction or a reconstruction. "The de- of deconstruction," as Derrida has said quite explicitly (and on more than one occasion), "signifies not the demolition of what is constructing itself, but rather what remains to be thought beyond the constructionist or destructionist schema."[10] Deconstruction, therefore, identifies something entirely other than what is commonly understood

"Deconstruction" is not negative. The word does not indicate "to take apart," "to un-construct," or "to disassemble."

and delimited by the conceptual opposition situated between, for example, the assumed positive term "construction" and its negation "destruction."

Despite this explicit qualification, however, deconstruction has been routinely reabsorbed by and understood according to a construction vs. destruction schema. The practice of deconstructive criticism, as the name implies, (mis)appropriated the term "deconstruction" to the task and project of literary criticism, turning it into, as Derrida describes, a "methodology for reading and for interpretation" and thereby becoming "domesticated by academic institutions."[11] As J. Hillis Miller acerbically explained in the final essay of what is considered to be the defining textbook of deconstructive criticism:

> The word "deconstruction," has misleading
> overtones or implications. It suggests something
> a bit too external. . . . It suggests the demolition
> of the helpless text with tools which are other
> than and stronger than what is demolished. The
> word "deconstruction" suggests that such criticism
> is an activity turning something unified back to
> detached fragments or parts. It suggests the image
> of a child taking apart his father's watch, reducing it
> back to useless parts, beyond any reconstitution.
> A deconstructionist is not a parasite but a parricide.

He is a bad son demolishing beyond hope of repair the machine of Western metaphysics.[12]

Gayatri Chakravorty Spivak, who translated Derrida's *De la grammatologie* into English, identifies this institutionalized (mis)appropriation as "a localized historical paradox." As she explains: "Deconstruction in the narrow sense domesticates deconstruction in the general sense. It is thus that it fits into the existing ideology of American literary criticism."[13] Whether this distinction between a *general* and *specific* sense of deconstruction is sufficient to account for the difference that separates the original concept (which, as we have seen, is already not original) from its subsequent (mis)application in American literary criticism is itself something that obsessed an entire generation of scholars and was the subject of deconstruction.

Similarly the word—mainly because it was, for better or worse, considered trendy or fashionable in the later part of the twentieth century—has been appropriated, repurposed, and deployed across a number of different fields and endeavors. The theoretical physicist Brian Greene, for instance, breaks down and examines the original components of the physical universe under the title "Deconstructing the Bang." Stephen P. Stich reevaluates recent developments in cognitive science by *Deconstructing the Mind*. In the book *Deconstructing Developmental Psychology*, Erica Burman takes up and uses the word as a kind of critical method for laying bare and reevaluating the processes and procedures of her discipline. And in *Deconstructing Special Education and Constructing Inclusion*, Gary Thomas and Andrew Loxley take apart the conceptual apparatus of special education programs.[14]

The term "deconstruction" has also found application beyond these academic disciplines, where it has been used as another name for decomposition, reverse engineering, or disassembly. Steve Ettlinger, for instance, examines the constitutive components of junk food in *Twinkie, Deconstructed: My Journey to Discover How the Ingredients Found in Processed Foods Are Grown, Mined (Yes, Mined), and Manipulated into What America Eats*. Mohammad Rahman dissects and investigates the inner workings of a popular computer language in the book *C# Deconstructed: Discover How C# Works on the .NET Framework*. In the world of fashion, there is *Ript It!*, in which Elissa Meyich explains "how to deconstruct and reconstruct the clothes of your dreams," Bridgett Artise and Jen Karetnick's *Born-Again Vintage: 25 Ways to Deconstruct, Reinvent, and Recycle Your Wardrobe*, and Alison Gill's "Deconstruction Fashion: The Making of Unfinished, Decomposing and Re-assembled Clothes."[15] Likewise, in the field of building construction, the word "deconstruction" is now routinely used to identify an alternative strategy to demolition: "Bulldozing a house and burying the shattered structure in a hole in the ground sounds perverse . . . an alternative is deconstruction, which simply means systematically dismantling a building and salvaging its parts for reuse."[16]

In politics, Steve Bannon, one-time chief strategist for President Donald Trump, characterized the main objective of the Trump administration as being "the deconstruction of the administrative state," by which he meant the dismantlement of regulatory agencies and other bureaucratic offices in U.S. federal government. And in the arts, there is Woody Allen's 1997 feature film *Deconstructing Harry*, a number of film reviews in the *New York Times* with titles like "The Many Faces of 'Black Swan,' Deconstructed," "Deconstructing the Realities of Politics and Terrorism," and "A Paleontologist Deconstructs 'Jurassic World.'"[17] There are also film school courses with names like "Deconstructing the Sound Track" and "Deconstructing Film Lighting." In music, there is Scott Freiman's lecture series *Deconstructing the Beatles*, in which the musicologist provides fans with an inside look at how the band's landmark albums and hit songs were made. And in the culinary arts, celebrity chefs, like Graham Elliot, (dis)assemble "deconstructed salads" by arranging separate piles of greens, vegetables, and dressing on a plate.[18]

In these contexts and situations, the word "deconstruction" comes to be repurposed, reformulated, and redeployed through misunderstandings, mischaracterizations, or mistranslations that have the effect of transforming deconstruction into something that it explicitly is not. Interestingly, this has been both an advantage and a problem. It is precisely because of these various appropriations and reformulations that deconstruction—the word and the concept—became popular and well known. When we look at the distribution of the word in books published in the English language (by way of the Ngram Viewer from Google Books), there is a remarkable proliferation beginning around the year 1980 and continuing through 1998, after which occurrences begin to drop off and plateau (figure 1).

The exponential increase in the number of published texts containing the word "deconstruction" is due, in large part, to the (mis)appropriations and domestications of the word across many different fields and contexts during the final decades of the twentieth century. Even though these different reuses are—technically speaking—incorrect, inaccurate, or inattentive, they have nevertheless made a

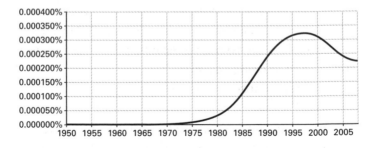

Figure 1 Changes over time for occurrences of the word "deconstruction" in books published in English. From Google Books Ngram Viewer.

positive contribution to the word's popularity and recognized street cred. At the same time, however, it is also due to this seemingly unrestrained proliferation, where deconstruction comes to identify all kinds of different activities depending on the context in which it is repurposed, that the word and the concept become increasingly diluted and difficult to define. Its popularity, therefore, has been both a blessing and a curse.

Deconstruction Is Not Analysis or Critique

In many fields, deconstruction—in terms of what Spivak calls "the specific sense"—has been defined and characterized by associating it with other activities one is already familiar with, specifically analysis and criticism. And this has proceeded, for better or worse, despite and in direct opposition to explicit statements to the contrary: "Deconstruction is neither an analysis nor a critique."[19] This is because both terms are inappropriate synonyms. Let's break this down further, or, perhaps more accurately stated, analyze how and critique why deconstruction is not and cannot be just another name for *analysis* or *critique*.

The word "analysis" is of Greek origin and refers to "breaking up, loosening, or unraveling." Analysis, in other words, is the process of breaking apart a composite structure in order to identify and isolate the smaller, constitutive parts that comprise the whole. The word has been in circulation for centuries and, for that reason, has recognizable application and significance in many different fields. In the natural sciences, for example, "chemical analysis" describes the process of determining the individual properties of a chemical compound by breaking down the composite substance into its fundamental components—for example, water consists of hydrogen and oxygen. With literature, music, film, or other forms of artwork, analysis describes a method of interpretation or way of understanding the work—such as a story, a symphony, a film—by identifying and isolating the individual components that together make up the whole. And in engineering and design, analysis is often visually presented in the form of block diagrams, flowcharts, and process models that show the individual components and their points of contact and interaction with each other.

But deconstruction is not analysis, and Derrida is quite direct and emphatic on this point. The process, values, and objectives of analysis—namely, the decomposition, dissection, and reduction of some larger whole into its simple, fundamental components—is itself something that is to be deconstructed. In other words, what deconstruction deconstructs (if one may be permitted this kind of recursive statement) is the conceptual difference that distinguishes part from whole, simple from complex, and assembly from decomposition. Instead of being another name for analysis, deconstruction critically reevaluates the fundamental arrangement and operations of any and all forms of analysis.

Likewise deconstruction is not just another name for criticism, and Derrida is just as quick to put distance between deconstruction and what is typically called "critique." The English word "critique" is derived from an ancient Greek word, which denotes "to separate," "to discern," or "to cut (apart)." In contemporary usage, the word has at least two meanings. In its general and colloquial sense, the word commonly has a negative connotation, indicating a form of judgmental evaluation or fault finding typically undertaken to identify flaws and imperfections. Criticism, in this sense, is often mobilized as another name for troubleshooting or debugging—the process of identifying problems in order fix them.

There is, however, another definition of the term that is rooted in the traditions and practices of critical philosophy. As Barbara Johnson characterizes it, criticism is not simply an examination of a particular system's flaws and imperfections designed to make it better. Instead, "it is an analysis that focuses on the grounds of that system's possibility. The critique reads backwards from what seems natural, obvious, self-evident, or universal, in order to show that these things have their history, their reasons for being the way they are, their effects on what follows from them, and that the starting point is not a given but a construct, usually blind to itself."[20] Understood in this way, criticism does not simply aim to discern problems in order to fix them or ask questions in order to provide readymade solutions. There is, of course, nothing inherently wrong with such a practice. Strictly speaking, however, criticism involves more. It consists in an examination that seeks to identify and expose a particular system's fundamental operations and conditions of possibility, demonstrating how what initially appears to be beyond question and entirely obvious does, in fact, possess a complex history that not only influences what proceeds from it, but also is itself often not recognized as such.

As useful as both senses of "critique" are and have been in various intellectual pursuits and activities, deconstruction is not critical. Instead, the activity of critique—whether that is understood in terms of an effort at troubleshooting or in the more precise sense developed in the critical philosophy of Immanuel Kant and others—is "one of the essential 'themes' or 'objects' of deconstruction."[21] As is the case with analysis, deconstruction is not critique; critique is one of the targets or sites/occasions of deconstruction.

Deconstruction Is Not a Method

Following from this, we can also say that deconstruction is not a *method* that would be situated alongside other kinds of research protocols and procedures. Derrida again is emphatic on this point: "Deconstruction is not a method and cannot be transformed into one."[22] This is because methods, as Rodolphe Gasché explains, "are generally understood as roads (from *hodos*: 'way,' 'road') to knowledge. In the sciences—as well as in the philosophies that scientific thinking patronizes—method is an instrument for representing a given field, and it is applied to the field from the outside."[23] Conceptualized in this fashion, methods are both instrumental and subjective.

Methods are instrumental in that they describe a standard procedure or set of discrete steps that can be followed for producing a particular outcome. "A good method," as J. Hillis Miller explains in his book *For Derrida*, "follows after a track implicitly already laid out as a sure way to get where you want to go, that is, to a goal that is already there, waiting for you to get there."[24] The *scientific method*, for instance, describes a standard procedure for generating empirically verifiable knowledge. And within each scientific discipline—whether a natural, applied, or human science—there are sets of recognizable research methods that can be followed for the purpose of achieving new insights and knowledge in that field. But let's keep things really simple and work with a less esoteric example. A recipe describes a method for making a cake. If one follows the steps or procedures that are described in the text of the recipe, this should result in the achievement of a particular goal: the production of a cake. The recipe can be (and must be) formulated and describe in generalizable terms outside of and prior to the actual application of those procedures in any particular circumstance or with any particular set of materials.

Understood as the instrumental means to an end, methods are also something selected, deployed, and applied by someone to something. In the case of scientific research, this someone would be the researcher or research team that decides which of the available methods is the most appropriate instrument given the object of investigation and then, as active subjects, applies the selected method to the designated object. In the case of a cake, for example, this role would be occupied by the baker, who applies the method, in other words, the recipe, to a set of ingredients and, in doing so, produces the end product: the cake. Like any instrument or tool, methods are nothing and do nothing by themselves. They are only useful and able to be used for some outcome, when taken up and properly employed by some active subject.

Deconstruction, however, does not admit to this kind of abstraction and formalization. As Derrida explains, "Deconstruction does not exist somewhere, pure, proper, self-identical, outside of its inscriptions in conflictual and differentiated contexts; it 'is' only what it does and what is done with it, there where it takes place."[25] Consequently, there is no one single or univocal deconstruction, but only specific and irreducible instances in which deconstruction takes place. Unlike a method, which is able to be generalized in advance of its particular applications, deconstruction comprises a highly specific form of involvement that is context dependent and particular. It is for this reason that deconstruction (which, if we are really strict about things, should probably be written in the plural) cannot be "reduced to some methodological instrumentality or to a set of rules and transposable procedures."[26] Likewise, it cannot be formulated as an act or an operation that is selected, directed, and controlled by a subject. "Deconstruction," as Derrida asserts in his third lecture memorializing Paul de Man, "cannot be applied, after the fact and from the outside, as a technical instrument."[27] Or as J. Hillis Miller explains, using the culinary metaphor of the recipe, "deconstruction is not an all-purpose tool that deconstructs every system in the same way, like a recipe for cooking all fish, flesh, or fowl identically."[28]

For these reasons, deconstruction is a kind of anti- or non-method. As Derrida explains, "It does not settle for methodical procedures, it opens up a passageway, it marches ahead and marks a trail."[29] Deconstruction, then, is less a *method* and more of what the Brazilian philosopher of communication Ciro Marcondes Filho has called "*metáporo*." According to Marcondes Filho, a method is, "by definition, a pre-mapped path that the researcher needs to follow." It is, therefore, generally "fixed, rigid, and immutable." By contrast, *metáporo* is more flexible and responsive to the particular: "If on the contrary, one opts for a procedure that follows its object and accompanies it in its unfolding, this opens a way, a 'poros' or a furrow, like a boat that cuts through the water without creating tracks. With *metáporo*, the object follows its own way and we accompany it without previous *script*, without a predetermined route, living in what happens while pursing the investigation."[30] Deconstruction, then, is not a tool or instrument of investigation that is selected, taken up, and utilized by a (human) subject and applied to an object of knowledge. One does not, for instance, wake up in the morning, go to the office, and get to work deconstructing some object or another. Rather, the object of deconstruction is always and already in deconstruction such that the task of the human subject is to accompany or follow its particular unfoldings. The subject, therefore, is subject(ed) to the object(ive) of deconstruction.

Despite direct and quite explicit statements to the contrary, however, deconstruction has been subject to repeated and persistent efforts to turn it into a method of investigation. Paradoxically, Derrida not only acknowledged this but also, despite his own statements to the contrary, was often complicit in these methodological transformations. "It is true," Derrida notes, "that in certain circles (university or cultural, especially in the United States) the technical and methodological 'metaphor' that seems

The object of deconstruction is always and already in deconstruction such that the task of the human subject is to accompany or follow its particular unfoldings.

necessarily attached to the very word 'deconstruction' has been able to seduce or lead astray."[31] For this reason, it is not uncommon to come across formulations like "the method of deconstruction" or "deconstructionism." And this has been particularly evident in the fields of literary theory and criticism, where (and, as Derrida explicitly remarks, "especially in the United States") deconstruction was not just a method for doing literary criticism. It became a recognizable school of thought. The Yale School, as it was called, had been "a shorthand way of referring to a moment in the 1970s when the work of Jacques Derrida was taken up and experimented with by four prominent literary critics in the Department of English at Yale: Paul de Man, J. Hillis Miller, Geoffrey H. Hartman, and Harold Bloom."[32]

Paul de Man (1919–1983), who was at that time arguably the best known and most visible of literary critics at Yale, characterized the method of deconstructive criticism in the following way: "Deconstruction is not something we have added to the text but it constituted the text in the first place. A literary text simultaneously asserts and denies the authority of its own rhetorical mode, and by reading the text as we did we were only trying to come closer to being a rigorous a reader as the author had to be in order to write the sentence in the first place."[33] For de Man, deconstruction was theorized, practiced, and taught as a particular way of reading. Unlike other forms of literary criticism, which often bring or add something to the text from the outside, the deconstructive reading sought to identify and trace the play of tensions that comprise the very texture of the work. As Jonathan Culler explained a decade later in a book that has served as something of a handbook for deconstructive criticism: "deconstruction does not elucidate texts in the traditional sense of attempting to grasp a unifying content or theme; it investigates the work of metaphysical oppositions in their arguments and the ways in which textual figures and relations . . . produce a double, aporetic logic."[34]

Similar kinds of statements—what Wlad Godzich called, in an essay critical of de Man, "the domestication of Derrida"[35]—can be found in the writings of other deconstructivists. Barbara Johnson, who was one of de Man's PhD students at Yale and the translator of Derrida's book *Dissemination*, described the theory and practice this way: "Deconstruction is not a form of textual vandalism designed to prove that meaning is impossible. In fact, the word 'deconstruction' is closely related not to the word 'destruction' but to the word 'analysis,' which etymologically means 'to undo'—a virtual synonym for 'to deconstruct.'"[36] In this statement, Johnson actually goes further than either de Man or Culler, describing deconstruction as a virtual synonym for literary analysis, the objective of which is the "careful teasing out of warring forces of signification within the text."[37]

Consequently, even when (and in direct opposition to what Derrida had specified) it comes to be transformed into a method, deconstruction is not one well-defined theory/practice but remains multifaceted, diverse, and differentiated. These differences—what one might call, following Johnson, the "warring forces" within Yale School itself—were evident and on display in the 1979 book that was widely considered to be the manifesto of the movement, *Deconstruction and Criticism*. In the introduction to this collection (which included essays from Harold Bloom, Paul de Man, Jacques Derrida, Geoffrey H. Hartman, J. Hillis Miller), Hartman distinguished between what he called the "boa-deconstructors"—represented by de Man, Derrida, and Miller—who pursue a merciless project of "disclosing again and again the 'abysm' of words" and the other critics, like Hartman and Bloom, who are "barely deconstructionists" and even critical of the effort.[38]

The development of deconstructive criticism at Yale University and elsewhere (in 1986, Miller left Yale and moved the center of gravity to the University of California Irvine) is another one of those ambivalent outcomes that can be considered both positive and negative. On the one hand, the transformation of deconstruction into a method of reading and an identifiable school of thought is something that has clearly benefited Derrida—the man, his published works, and his international reputation. Without this (mis)appropriation or domestication—which

Derrida both participated in (insofar as he contributed an essay to *Deconstruction and Criticism*) and had directly criticized and opposed—it is quite certain that deconstruction would not have been as popular as it was nor would Derrida and his writings been highly sought-after targets for academic meetings, visiting professorships, and translation efforts. Consequently, even if the method of deconstructive criticism is fundamentally wrong or misguided, it had an important and lasting impact.

On the other hand, this domestication of deconstruction was something that had been routinely lampooned and criticized in both the academic and popular press of the time. In "Deconstructing Deconstruction," a book review of both the Yale School manifesto *Deconstruction and Criticism* and Paul de Man's *Allegories of Reading*, Denis Donoghue provided the following, rather scathing diagnosis: "I think Deconstruction appeals to the clerisy of graduate students, who like to feel themselves superior to the laity of common readers, liberated from their shared meanings; liberated, too, from the tedious requirement of meaning as such, the official obligation to suppose that words mean something finite rather than everything or nothing."[39] Six year later, in 1986, the *New York Times* published a critical reappraisal of the entire movement of deconstructive criticism under the title "The Tyranny of the Yale Critics." "What is deconstruction? To 'deconstruct' a text is pretty much what it sounds like—to pick the thing carefully apart, exposing what deconstructors see as the central fact and tragic little secret of Western philosophy—namely, the circular tendency of language to refer to itself. Because the 'language' of a text refers mainly to other 'languages' and texts—and not to some hard, extra-textual reality—the text tends to have several possible meanings, which usually undermine one another."[40]

The disciplining of deconstruction—its transformation by a particular discipline into a method of disciplinary practice—did have important consequences, which are perhaps only now apparent in retrospect. It was largely due to the fact that deconstruction did became a method (or, if one prefers, a quasi-method) that the term came to have significance and was recognized as such. Without this domestication or what Jeffrey Nealon has called "the commodification of deconstruction in America,"[41] deconstruction might have remained little more than a footnote concerning the translation of a technical word in the work of Heidegger. But once domesticated, commodified, and "simplified and watered down for use in how-to books,"[42] it became a target for criticism not only from Derrida, who time and again spoke out and struggled against the transformation, but from others who, in conflating what Derrida had called "deconstruction" with what had become the method of deconstructive criticism, saw (or perhaps better stated "thought they saw") a profound threat and a challenge to the status quo. As Johnson explains in an essay titled "Nothing Fails Like Success": "As soon as any radically innovative thought becomes an *ism*, its specific ground breaking force diminishes, its historical notoriety increases, and its disciples tend to become more simplistic, more dogmatic, and ultimately more conservative, at which time its power becomes institutional rather than analytical."[43] Such was the fate of deconstruction in America.[44]

Deconstruction Is Not (Just) Discourse Analysis

One byproduct of the proliferation and relative success of deconstructive criticism (not only but especially within the United States) is that it has led to the conclusion that deconstruction is an elite and heady academic thing limited to ivory-tower intellectuals. This is, on the one hand, not necessarily inaccurate or insignificant. As Simon Crichley explains, "The first essential point to make, however trivial it may seem, is that deconstruction is always deconstruction of a *text*. Derrida's thinking is always thinking *about* a text, from which flows the obvious corollary that deconstruction is always engaged in *reading* a text."[45] On the other hand, and at the same time, Derrida also recognized and affirmed the need to extend deconstruction beyond the limits of discourse analysis: "Deconstruction is not, should not be only an analysis of discourse, of philosophical statements or concepts, of a semantics; it has to challenge institutions, social and political structures, the most hardened traditions."[46] This desire to open deconstruction to the wider challenge of "the most hardened of traditions" is perhaps best illustrated and exemplified by the way deconstruction interfaces with the hardened traditions, concrete materials, and subject matter of architecture.

During the mid-1980s, deconstruction became increasingly tangled up in the subject matter and materials of architecture. The American architect Peter Eisenman began using the word "deconstruction" to describe and promote his own design work. And Derrida himself became directly involved with architecture by way of personal and professional interactions with Eisenman, Bernard Tschumi, and Daniel Libeskind. This was not, at least not as Derrida understood and explained, a simple appropriation or domestication of deconstruction. "When I read certain texts written by those in the milieu of Tschumi and Eisenman about their architecture and their projects . . . I at first thought naively of a sort of analogic transposition or application. And then I realized . . . that was not at all what was going on, and that, in fact, what they are doing under the name of deconstructive architecture was the most literal and most intense affirmation of deconstruction."[47]

This "intense affirmation" eventually produces a recognizable architectural style, codified and publicized by way of an influential Museum of Modern Art (MoMA) exhibition from 1988 called *Deconstructivist Architecture*. As described by the exhibition's curators Mark Wigley and Philip Johnson, "This is an architecture of disruption, dislocation, deflection, deviation, and distortion, rather than one of demolition, decay, decomposition, or disintegration. It displaces structure instead of destroying it."[48] Notably, the exhibition did not try to define and defend a singular style of deconstructivism but brought together seven internationally known architects whose work, in one way or another, exemplified this unorthodox approach to design in an "uneasy alliance"—Coop Himmelb(l)au, Peter Eisenman, Frank Gehry, Zaha M. Hadid, Rem Koolhaas, Daniel Libeskind, and Bernard Tschumi.

Deconstruction, despite initial appearances, is not, at least not exclusively, a heady academic exercise of reading texts that is practiced at elite institutions of higher education. It is—or it was at least understood to be—a wider ranging, general mode of intervention in existing structures and institutions. If deconstruction were limited to discourse analysis or critical theory, then it would have remained the captive of a particular literary undertaking during a specific historical moment and may not be able to address itself to the opportunities and challenge of life in the twenty-first century. In fact, as Michael Naas has argued, this, more than anything else, is the contemporary challenge or opportunity for deconstruction: "For deconstruction can continue to work today only by being repeated, reread in its letter, and transplanted elsewhere, uprooted and translated into other idioms, grafted onto other contexts, reformatted according to other protocols, taken out of its original context and sometimes, brought closer to 'home.'"[49] And it was arguably in architecture that deconstruction found itself closer to home, even if that home remained essentially *unheimlich*.[50]

Outcomes and Results

If we are being honest with ourselves, it is hard to deny that this chapter has had the effect of deconstructing— understood in the specific, domesticated, commodified, or derived sense of the word—all the ways the term and the concept of *deconstruction* have been misconstrued, misappropriated, or mistranslated. In this process of deconstructing deconstruction,[51] we have strategically appropriated and deliberately dissembled the wrong formulations of the term in order to break down, take apart, disassemble, analyze, or critique what amounts to erroneous and mistaken characterizations, appropriations, and domestications of the word.

This curious reduplication turns out to be something of a standard operating procedure in philosophy since at least the time of Plato. As Derrida points out in his reading of the *Phaedrus*, "Plato imitates the imitators in order to restore the truth of what they imitate: namely, truth itself."[52] But these recursive gestures of reusing the negative against itself do not (at least not in and by themselves), produce or reveal a positive outcome. In explaining what deconstruction is not, has never been, and should not become, very little (virtually nothing, in fact) has been said about what deconstruction is or, perhaps more accurately stated, how it would transpire or take place. Chapter 3 will respond to this deficiency by providing a more affirmative and informative characterization.

DECONSTRUCTING DECONSTRUCTION

So far, all we know is what deconstruction is not, should not be confused with, or must not be assumed to have been. In a nutshell,[1] deconstruction is not the opposite of construction, nor is it a synonym for or another way to say destruction, demolition, or disassembly. If it is none of these, then what is it? This question—although seemingly direct and standard operating procedure for this kind of effort—is already mistaken or misdirected, insofar as the very grammatical and logical form of the propositional statement "S is P" is itself something that will have been submitted to deconstruction. So, to reorient the direction of the inquiry, we can formulate the question in a different fashion: How does deconstruction transpire or take place?

Although Derrida has responded to this question in a number of places, the most complete and succinct presentation was provided in the course of an interview with

Jean-Louis Houdebine and Guy Scarpetta, published in 1971. In the course of this conversation, Derrida reflects on his own efforts and provides the following explanation: "What interested me then, that I am attempting to pursue along other lines now, was, at the same time as a 'general economy,' a kind of general strategy of deconstruction. The latter is to avoid both simply neutralizing the binary oppositions of metaphysics and simply residing within the closed field of these oppositions, thereby confirming it."[2] If we break this down, take it apart, or analyze it—if we, in a word, "deconstruct" it, to redeploy what would by comparison need to be characterized as the wrong (or the insufficient or vulgar) sense of the word—we can extract and identify several important features.

Binary Opposition

Deconstruction names a strategy—what Derrida calls a "general strategy"—by which to engage with and respond to "the binary oppositions of metaphysics." So let's work backward, beginning with those binary oppositions. We will eventually return to and pick up the "general strategy" part, which is not insignificant. In the opening salvo of *Beyond Good and Evil*, Friedrich Nietzsche had pointed out that "the fundamental faith of the metaphysicians is the belief in opposite values."[3] These opposite values are formulated and expressed in terms of conceptual opposites or mutually exclusive predicates: being/nothing, inside/outside, mind/body, male/female, self/other, light/dark, natural/artificial, and so on. "All metaphysicians," Derrida writes, "from Plato to Rousseau, Descartes to Husserl, have proceeded in this way, conceiving good to be before evil, the positive before the negative, the pure before the impure, the simple before the complex, the essential before the accidental, the imitated before the imitation, etc. And this is not just one metaphysical gesture among others, it is the metaphysical exigency."[4] This is not, we should note, just a logical quirk of something called "metaphysics." As Derrida explains in conversation with Julia Kristeva, even "everyday language" is the language of metaphysics.[5] In other words, we typically make sense of ourselves and our world by deploying sets of terminological differences or binary oppositions. As Barbara Johnson explains, the underlying logic of this way of thinking—that is to say, "If not absolute, then relative; if not objective then subjective; if you are not for something; you are against it"—is the principle of noncontradiction.[6]

This principle, or what is also called the "law of noncontradiction," at least since the time of Aristotle has been one of the defining conditions—if not *the* defining condition—of human knowledge. As Paula Gottlieb explains in the *Stanford Encyclopedia of Philosophy* entry for the subject: "According to Aristotle, first philosophy, or metaphysics, deals with ontology and first principles, of which the principle (or law) of noncontradiction is the firmest. Aristotle says that without the principle of non-contradiction we could not know anything that we do know."[7] As proof of this, we only need to consider what has already transpired here: We have (perhaps without even acknowledging it as such) employed this basic principle in the process of defining deconstruction by way of distinguishing it from what it is not.

Deconstruction takes aim at and intervenes in this logical order in a way that neither confirms nor opposes it.[8] To *confirm* this logical order would be to leave it as is and not question, obstruct, or interfere with its operations in any way. But to *oppose* it—despite what one might initially think—would result in the same, insofar as any effort to push back against or resist this way of thinking already takes place and deploys the very logical operation that would be opposed or resisted in the first place. "It is impossible," as Jean Baudrillard explains, "to destroy the system by a contradiction-based logic or by reversing the balance of forces—in short, by a direct, dialectical revolution affecting the economic or political infrastructure. Everything that produces contradiction or a balance of forces or energy in general merely feeds back into the system and drives it on."[9] When it comes to binary oppositions, resistance appears to be futile. Any form of opposition or critical pushback would already and immediately become reabsorbed into the very system that one would be seeking to oppose and work against. For this reason, it remains persistently difficult to say anything against, to disrupt, or even question the hegemony of binary opposition without already participating in and utilizing the very terminology and logic that were to be submitted to scrutiny in the first place.

Structuralism

This systemic or structural problem was something that had been identified and theorized in structuralism, a twentieth-century intellectual development that found application in fields as diverse as linguistics, anthropology, literary theory, sociology, and philosophy. Although "structuralism" does not name a formal discipline or singular method of investigation, its innovations are widely recognized as the result of developments in the structural linguistics of Ferdinand de Saussure.

In the posthumously published *Course in General Linguistics*, Saussure argued for a fundamental shift in the way that language is understood and analyzed. "The common view," as Jonathan Culler describes it, "is doubtless that a language consists of words, positive entities, which are put together to form a system and thus acquire relations with one another."[10] Saussure turns this common-sense view on its head. For him, the fundamental element of language is the sign and the formal structure of the sign is opposition or difference. "In language," Saussure argues in one of his work's most often quoted passages, "there are only differences. Even more important: a difference generally implies positive terms between which the difference is set up; but in language there are only differences *without positive terms*."[11] For Saussure, then, language is not composed of linguistic units that have some intrinsic value or positive meaning and that subsequently comprise a system of language through their interrelationships. Instead, a sign, any sign in any language, is defined by the differences that distinguish it from other signs within the linguistic system to which it belongs.

The dictionary provides what is perhaps the best illustration of this basic semiotic principle. As Jay David Bolter explains: "We can only define a sign in terms of other signs of the same nature. This lesson is known to every child who discovers that fundamental paradox of the dictionary: that if you do not know what some words mean you can never use the dictionary to learn what other words mean. The definition of any word, if pursued far enough through the dictionary, will lead you in circles."[12] Signs, therefore, do not refer to things that exist outside the system of signs; signs refer to other signs. Although this concept was already mobilized and developed in Plato's

Cratylus, it is the dictionary that provides an easily accessible illustration. In a dictionary, words are defined by other words, typically synonyms or antonyms of the word to be defined. In pursuing definitions of words in the dictionary, one remains within the system of linguistic signifiers and never gets outside language to the referent or what semioticians call the "transcendental signified."

According to this way of thinking, the linguistic sign is not a positive term, it is an effect of difference, and language (any language) is a system of differences. This characterization of language, although never explicitly described in this fashion by Saussure, mirrors the logic of the digital computer, where the binary digits 0 and 1 have no intrinsic or positive meaning but are simply indicators and an effect of difference—a switch that is either on or off. If structuralism is right (or at least accurate on this point), then binary opposition does not just describe the technical operations of the digital computer but also characterizes the fundamental structure of language and human cognition, meaning that it is not possible to conceptualize or to say anything about binary opposition without utilizing and participating in the system or logical order it organizes. This is one aspect of the meaning that is conveyed by what remains one of the most famous (or notorious) statements from Derrida: "*Il n'y a pas de hors-texte*" or "There is nothing outside the text."[13]

It is not possible
to conceptualize or
to say anything about
binary opposition
without utilizing and
participating in the
system or logical order
it organizes.

Between a Rock and a Hard Place

Binary oppositions are undoubtedly useful and expedient. Daniel Chandler (who wrote the basic book on semiotics) argues that "people have believed in the fundamental character of binary oppositions since at least classical times" and that it would be difficult, if not impossible, to operate otherwise.[14] Peter Elbow suggests that "there's no hope of getting away from binary oppositions given the nature of the human mind and situation. Binary thinking seems to be the path of least resistance for the perceptual system, for thinking, and for linguistic structures. . . . It may be that the very structure of our bodies and our placement in phenomenal reality invite us to see things in terms of binary oppositions."[15] And Aristotle argued that the principle of noncontradiction—the fact that it is impossible to think or say that something both *is* and *is not*—is the most indisputable of all principles and, therefore, beyond all possible demonstration or logical derivation.[16]

Despite the fact that this is both expedient and a seemingly inescapable principle of thought and language, there are problems. First, binary oppositions restrict what is possible to know and to say about the world and our own experiences. This is because opposites push things toward the extremes. In this either/or mode, any given phenomenon is assumed to be reducible to *x* or its opposite, *not-x*. Although this kind of exclusivity has a certain functionality and logical attraction, it often is not entirely in touch with the complexity and exigency of things on the ground. Recent efforts to mobilize more accurate descriptions of personal identity, for instance, strain against the restrictions that have been instituted and imposed, for example, by the exclusive gender binary of male/female. For this reason, binary opposites often seem to be unable to represent accurately or to capture the rich experiences of empirical reality, which always seems to complicate simple division into one of two options. It is for this reason that we are generally critical of "false dichotomies"—the parsing of complex reality into a simple either/or distinction. There are, therefore, both ontological and epistemological reasons to question the hegemony of binary oppositions and the limitations that they impose.

Second, conceptual opposites arrange and exert power. For any logical opposition or binary pairing, the two items are not typically situated on a level playing field; one of the pair has already been determined to be the privileged term. Or as Derrida explains, "We are not dealing with the peaceful coexistence of a *vis-à-vis*, but rather with a violent hierarchy. One of the two terms governs the other (axiologically, logically, etc.), or has the upper hand."[17] With the standard gender distinction situated between the two terms "male" and "female," for example, it is the male who is considered, from the book of *Genesis* to psychoanalysis and beyond, to be the original and basic form of the human species. In the Judeo-Christian creation myth, for instance, it is the man, Adam, who is created first, and the woman Eve is derived from him. Following this way of thinking, women have been routinely characterized as a derivative and negative counterpart. That is, the female typically has been described by what she lacks in comparison to the male. And this formulation—which, as noted earlier, Derrida termed "phallogocentrism"—has been leveraged to justify centuries of marginalization, oppression, and exclusion.

A similar, structural inequality has been identified with the terms that define conversation and debate about race in the United States and elsewhere. As W. Lawrence Hogue explains: "Within the white/black binary opposition in the West, the African American is defined as a devalued Other."[18] Formulated in this way, "white" is a privileged term and "black" is determined as its negative counterpart and other. To make matters worse, this already unequal arrangement—one that encodes prejudice in the very terms by which we think and speak of racial difference—often has been and remains invisible to those who benefit from this privilege. This comprises what is designated by the phrase "the invisibility of whiteness." It is for this reason, that racism is a structural matter and not just an empirical problem, in other words, the fact that there are individuals who have and express racist opinions or tell ethnic jokes. What is at stake in binary opposition, then, is not simply a manner of conveniently dividing up the world into this or that. Conceptual pairings—like male/female and white/black—no matter where they occur, or how they come to be arranged, always and already impose unequal distinctions and distributions of privilege and power.

Consequently, binary oppositions are not just a matter of discursive difference; they are the site of real social, political, and moral power. Whoever or whatever controls the terms of a debate controls the debate. Consider, for instance, how the abortion question has been structured in political discourse, especially in the United States. Each side in the dispute struggles to gain the upper hand by arranging a conceptual opposition in an attempt to govern how one thinks and speaks about this subject matter. One side designates itself "pro-life" in an effort to characterize its opponents as "anti-life." The other side calls itself "pro-choice" in order to define its adversary—the pro-life faction—as opponents of free choice, specifically a woman's right to choose. The political and moral debate about abortion, therefore (at least as it has transpired in the United States), is a struggle between two different sets of binary oppositions, each of which tries to get the upper hand in the conversation by controlling the very terms by which one thinks and speaks about abortion.

Binary oppositions, then, are neither neutral nor objective. They have real and potentially devastating

Binary oppositions are not just a matter of discursive difference; they are the site of real social, political, and moral power.

consequences. As Donna Haraway argues, "certain dualisms have been persistent in Western traditions; they have been systemic to the logics and practices of domination of women, people of color, nature, workers, animals—in short, domination of all constituted as others, whose task it is to mirror the self. Chief among these troubling dualisms are self/other, mind/body, culture/nature, male/female, civilized/primitive, reality/appearance, whole/part, agent/resource, maker/made, active/passive, right/wrong, truth/illusion, total/partial, God/man."[19] These logical distinctions, therefore, do not institute an equitable division between two terms that are on equal footing and of comparable status. They are always and already hierarchical arrangements that are structurally biased. And it is this skewed hierarchical order, as many feminists, environmentalists, postcolonial theorists, and others have demonstrated and documented, that installs, underwrites, and justifies systems of inequality, domination, and prejudice. There are, then, moral and political reasons to question systems of conceptual opposition and to attempt to think in excess of and beyond the usual and inherited arrangements. As Hannah Arendt concludes, "we all grow up and inherit a certain vocabulary. We then have got to examine this vocabulary."[20]

Finally, thinking and speaking in this way is not optional. Because of these profound systemic problems, there are good reasons to challenge the hegemony of binary opposition. But doing so is difficult, if not exceedingly impossible. Organizing things in terms of logical opposites does not appear to be a choice or a matter of individual volition. It is, as Nietzsche had pointed out, the "fundamental faith" that underlies and empowers all modes of thinking, up to and including that by which one would endeavor to question and to criticize it as such. Consequently, organizing things in terms of logical opposition, whether indicated by the name "dualism," "oppositional logic," "digital," "dichotomy," or "principle of noncontradiction," is not a choice or a matter of individual volition. One does not, for example, decide to think in terms of oppositional logic or not, which is obviously just one more binary opposition.

Consider, for example, one of the proposed solutions to the gender binary that has been advanced in the context of discussions concerning the rights of transgender and gender fluid individuals. Gender identity, it has been argued, does not easily accommodate itself to the existing rules of the game—the duality of male or female. In response to this, there have been efforts to articulate an alternative to the male/female binary. One possible alternative has been called "nonbinary," which immediately, and not surprisingly, produces another duality or binary opposition: nonbinary vs. binary. This is the thoroughly insidious and seemingly inescapable nature of the problem: opposing binary opposition by deploying the usual strategies of contradiction, reversal, or revolution not only does little or nothing to challenge the basic structure of the dominant system, but also is actually involved with and contributes to what one had wanted to oppose or criticize in the first place. As Audre Lorde accurately formulated the problem: "The master's tools will never dismantle the master's house."[21] But what other tools are there? How is it possible to say anything at all about that which ruptures and exceeds the limits of available words and concepts without (re)using those very words and concepts?

Poststructuralism

Binary oppositions are a problem. But directly opposing binary opposition is already part and parcel of the problem. This does not mean, however, that such structures and formations are simply beyond inquiry or constitute some kind of inescapable *fait accompli*, to which one must and can only surrender. It does not, it is important to note, simply disarm or render impotent any and all forms of intervention, whether political, social, philosophical, or otherwise. What it does mean, is that the engagement—if it is to be effective—will need to operate in excess of mere opposition and be structured in a way that is significantly different and otherwise. This is precisely what has been identified and assembled under the umbrella term "poststructuralism." As Mark Taylor explains: "While poststructuralism does not constitute a unified movement, writers as different as Jacques Derrida, Jacques Lacan, and Michel Foucault on the one hand, and on the other Hélène Cixous, Julia Kristeva, and Michel de Certeau devise alternative tactics to subvert the grid of binary oppositions with which structuralists believe they can capture reality."[22]

Since poststructuralism does not constitute a unified movement or singular method, what makes its different articulations cohere is not an underlying similarity but a difference, specifically different modes of thinking difference differently. In other words, what draws the different instances of poststructuralism together into loose affiliation that may be identified with this one term is not a homogeneous method or technique. Instead, what they share is a common interest in thinking the difference customarily situated between binary opposites outside of and beyond the grasp of structuralism's totalizing enclosure. Deconstruction, like other forms of poststructuralism, targets and seeks to disrupt the seemingly inescapable logic of noncontradiction. As Johnson explains: "Instead of a simple 'either/or' structure, deconstruction attempts to elaborate a discourse that says *neither* 'either/or,' *nor* 'both/and' nor even 'neither/nor,' while at the same time not totally abandoning these logics either."[23]

Although Taylor and others characterize and situate deconstruction under the banner of poststructuralism,[24] Derrida was not entirely comfortable with the label, and he deliberately complicated and questioned its suitability. The most direct formulation of this was provided in an essay titled "The Ends of Man" concerning what is typically called "philosophical anthropology." Here Derrida concludes by directly addressing what he terms "French thought" (aka "poststructuralism") calling out and cautioning against the two "false exits" that deconstruction has to negotiate and navigate between:

1. *Repetition*—"To attempt an exit and a deconstruction without changing terrain, by repeating what is implicit in the founding concepts and the original problematic, by using against the edifice the instruments or stones available in the house, that is, equally, in language. Here, one risks ceaselessly confirming, consolidating, *relifting* (*relever*), at an always more certain depth, that which one allegedly deconstructs."[25]

2. *Difference*—"To decide to change terrain, in a discontinuous and irruptive fashion, by brutally placing oneself outside, and by affirming an absolute break and difference . . . thereby inhabiting more naively and more strictly than ever the inside one declares to have deserted, the simple practice of language ceaselessly reinstates the new terrain on the oldest ground."[26]

Unlike other forms of poststructuralism, which Derrida criticizes for either remaining captive of the problematic one wishes to disrupt, or naively believing that one can simply break away and do something completely different and, in the process, unwittingly reinstating "the new terrain on the oldest ground"; deconstruction does something radically and disturbingly different.

Double Science

Deconstruction accomplishes this (or, perhaps more accurately stated, this comes to pass for deconstruction) by way of a double gesture. As Derrida explains in the course of the interview with Houdebine and Scarpetta: "We must proceed using a double gesture, according to a unity that is both systematic and in and of itself divided, according to a double writing, that is, a writing that is in and of itself multiple, what I called, in 'La double séance,' a double science."[27] This "double science" consists of two phases: *overturning* and *displacement*.

Overturning

The two terms that comprise a binary opposition are structurally arranged and formulated as an order of subordination, where one of the two terms already governs the other or has the upper hand. Deconstruction begins with a phase of overturning the existing hierarchy. This "flip-ping of the script," or what Derrida also describes as "bring low what was high"[28] is, quite literally, a *revolutionary* ges-ture insofar as the existing order—an arrangement that is already an unequal and violent hierarchy—is inverted or overturned. "To overlook this phase of overturning," Der-rida explains, "is to forget the conflictual and subordinat-ing structure of opposition."[29]

But inversion, in and by itself, is not sufficient. It is only half the story. And this is the reason why it is just a "phase" or the first step. As Derrida points out and is well aware (and he is following, among others, Nietzsche on this point) a conceptual inversion or revolutionary gesture—whether it be social, political, or philosophical—actually does little or nothing to challenge or change the dominant system. In merely exchanging the relative posi-tions occupied by the two opposed terms, inversion still maintains the binary opposition in which and on which it operates—albeit in reverse order or upside-down. Sim-ply turning things around, as Derrida notes, still "resides within the closed field of these oppositions, thereby con-firming it."[30]

Displacement
For this reason, deconstruction necessarily entails a sec-ond, post-revolutionary phase of displacement. "We must," as Derrida describes it, "also mark the interval between

inversion, which brings low what was high, and the irruptive emergence of a new 'concept,' a concept that can no longer be, and never could be, included in the previous regime."[31] Strictly speaking, this new concept is no concept whatsoever, for it always and already exceeds the system of dualities that define the conceptual order as well as the nonconceptual order with which the conceptual order has been articulated. It "can no longer be included within philosophical (binary) opposition, but which, however, inhabits philosophical opposition, resisting and disorganizing it, without ever constituting a third term, without ever leaving room for a solution in the form of speculative dialectics."[32]

This "new concept" that is the product of the second phase occupies a position between or in/at the margins of a traditional, conceptual opposition or binary pair. It is simultaneously neither-nor and either-or. It does not resolve into one or the other of the two terms that comprise the conceptual order, nor does it constitute a third term that would mediate their difference in a synthetic unity, as is the case with Hegelian dialectics (more on that follows). Consequently, it is positioned in such a way that it both inhabits and operates in excess of the conceptual oppositions by which and through which systems of knowledge have been organized and articulated. It is for this reason that the new concept cannot be described or marked in language, except (as is exemplified here) by engaging in what Derrida calls a "bifurcated writing," which compels the traditional philosophemes to articulate, however incompletely and insufficiently, what necessarily resists and displaces all possible modes of articulation.

Perhaps the best example and illustration of deconstruction's two-step operation is available with the term "deconstruction" itself. In a first move, deconstruction flips the script by putting emphasis on the negative term "destruction" as opposed to "construction." In fact, the apparent similitude between the two words, "deconstruction" and "destruction," is a deliberate and calculated aspect of this effort. But this is only step one—the phase of inversion. In the second phase of this double science, there is the emergence of a brand new and exorbitant concept. The novelty of this concept is marked, quite literally, in the material of the word itself. "Deconstruction," which is fabricated by combining the de- of "destruction" and attaching it to the opposite term "construction," produces a strange and disorienting neologism that does not fit in the existing order of things. It is an excessive and intentionally undecidable alternative that names a new possibility. This new concept, despite first appearances, is not negative. It is not the mere opposite of construction; rather, it exceeds the conceptual order instituted and regulated by the terminological opposition situated between construction and destruction. "It is only on this condition," Derrida concludes, "that deconstruction will provide itself the means with which to intervene in the field of oppositions that it criticizes."[33]

Nondialectical Third Term

When Derrida introduces and describes this third alternative that emerges from or in the process of deconstruction, he is very careful to distinguish it from the third term of Hegelian dialectics. This point of contact/differentiation is crucial. In fact, as Derrida explained, his entire philosophical enterprise could be described and contextualized in terms of an ongoing effort to respond to and to take responsibility for what remains of Hegel: "We will never be finished with the reading or rereading of Hegel, and, in a certain way, I do nothing other than attempt to explain myself on this point."[34]

Describing or characterizing Hegelian dialectics in the abstract is about as difficult as doing the same for deconstruction (which may, in fact, explain things). Hegel addressed this systemic problem explicitly and directly in the preface to *The Phenomenology of Spirit*: "Whatever might appropriately be said of philosophy in a preface—say a historical statement of the main drift and point of view, the general content and results, a string of random assertions and assurances about truth—none of this can be accepted as the way in which to expound philosophical truth."[35] For this reason, we will (again) proceed by beginning with what will turn out to be the wrong (or, at least, inaccurate or vulgar) formulation of the dialectic in order to approach what is a more accurate and attentive characterization.

Hegelian dialectics is typically mischaracterized as a dynamic process by which the tension between a thesis and its logical opposite or antithesis (aka a binary opposition) comes to be resolved by a third term, called the "synthesis." Although this "thesis-antithesis-synthesis" formula has been routinely attributed to Hegel and can readily be found in encyclopedia entries and textbooks, it actually does not appear, in this particular form, in any of Hegel's writings or published documents. In other words, "the Hegel legend of thesis-antithesis-synthesis" is just that, a legend.[36] It has little or no basis in Hegel's writings and is, in fact, the result of a misrepresentation and distortion of Hegelian philosophy.[37] Consequently, the thesis-antithesis-synthesis formula is not so much a characterization of Hegelian dialectics as it is a caricature.

The dialectic, as it is actually described by Hegel, consists not in the three substantive stages of thesis-antithesis-synthesis but in a dynamic process that is animated by two moments of *negation*. *The Science of Logic*, for instance, begins with *being*. Not any particular being but "being, pure being, without any further determination."[38] But in and by itself, this indeterminate first term means little or nothing. It comes to be determined through the process of differentiating itself from its opposite. This first negation, "by which the universal of the beginning of its own accord determines itself as the *other of itself*, is to be named the *dialectical* moment."[39] Being, for example, comes to be determined and differentiated through its negation, which is, not surprisingly, *nothing*.

The opposition of being and nothing, however, does not remain static and fixed as would be the case in the classic, Aristotelian logic of noncontradiction; it is itself overcome or negated. This "second negative," which is in fact the negative of a negative, is what Hegel calls the *Aufhebung* of the dialectical opposition.[40] Although usually translated by the rather archaic English word "sublation," *Aufhebung* names a unique operation, which Hegel argues is fundamental to all of philosophy. According to Hegel's characterization, "'*to sublate*' has a twofold meaning in language: on the one hand it means to preserve, to maintain, and equally it also means to cause to cease, to put an end to. . . . Thus what is sublated is at the same time preserved; it has only lost its immediacy but is not on that account annihilated."[41] The sublation of the logical opposition or dialectic of being and nothing, for instance, results in *becoming*. Becoming, therefore, constitutes a third term that both puts an end to the opposition of being and nothing and at the same time preserves their difference in itself. Or as Hegel describes it in that kind of dense prose for which he is famous: "*Becoming* is the unseparatedness of being and nothing, not the unity which abstracts from being and nothing; but as the unity of *being* and *nothing* it is this *determinate* unity in which there *is* both being and nothing."[42]

It is at this point that we can perceive the points of intersection and differentiation between Hegel's own description and the thesis-antithesis-synthesis caricature, which has, for better or worse, come to replace it. Hegel's description of the dialectic focuses attention on process and, in particular, the two moments of negation that animate or motivate it. For Hegel, what is initially *in-itself* is posited *for-itself* in the ordeal of the dialectical moment, and then becomes *in-* and *for-itself* through the unique activity of the *Aufhebung*. The thesis-antithesis-synthesis caricature, on the contrary, focuses attention not on the process but on the three substantive elements that are involved in this process. Although dedicated Hegelians argue that such a general and substantive description does not hold up across all the particular expressions of Hegel's philosophy, there is another point of differentiation that is equally if not more important.

When it is characterized substantively as involving three static components, one could get the mistaken impression that the dialectic has a simple end point. That is, thesis and antithesis are resolved by synthesis, which concludes the conflict and puts an end to the logical opposition.

For Hegel, however, the process is ongoing and cyclical. The result of sublation, what would ostensibly be the synthetic "third term," is not the end but is also a new beginning that immediately passes over into dialectical differentiation by positing its own negation in and by opposition to its other.[43] Consequently, the entirety of Hegelian philosophy "exhibits itself as a *circle* returning upon itself, the end being wound back to the beginning through the mediation; this circle is moreover a *circle of circles,* for each individual member as ensouled by the method is reflected into itself, so that in returning to the beginning it is at the same time the beginning of a new member."[44] Interestingly, this description, which accounts for both the points of intersection and differentiation between Hegelian philosophy and its legendary misrepresentation, performs the very thing that it seeks to describe. It does not simply differentiate Hegelian dialectics from the caricature of Hegelianism but sublates this difference and, in the process, produces what one might be tempted to call a "synthesis" of the two.

Deconstruction takes place and has its place as a kind of post-Hegelian thinking that aims to achieve escape velocity from the gravitational pull of Hegelian dialectics. I write "post" instead of "anti" (which is the term associated with other poststructuralists, such as Gilles Deleuze) because direct opposition to Hegel as the means of escaping the legacy and logic of Hegelianism is easier said than done. And it is one of Derrida's poststructuralist precursors, Michel Foucault, who provided what is quite possibly the most accurate articulation of the problem: "But to truly escape Hegel involves an exact appreciation of the price we have to pay to detach ourselves from him. . . . We have to determine the extent to which our anti-Hegelianism is possibly one of his tricks directed against us, at the end of which he stands motionless, waiting for us."[45]

Deconstruction, then, comprises a way to respond to and take responsibility for dialectical difference (Hegel's term), binary opposition (structuralism's formulation), or the principle of noncontradiction (Aristotelian logic) that can rupture and disturb the all-encompassing and seemingly inescapable closure of dialectics. Although other forms of poststructuralism sought to achieve the same objective, deconstruction is remarkably different. It proceeds by way of a two-step procedure or "double science," which comprises a kind of parody, perversion, or de-monstration of the dialectical process that results in the irruptive emergence of a third term that is not a dialectical resolution (or a synthesis) but remains disturbingly otherwise, exorbitant and/or monstrous. Deconstruction, therefore, designates a general strategy—perhaps the most sophisticated and potent of available strategies—for thinking outside the box, where "the box" is defined as the total enclosure and theoretical limit of what can be thought.[46]

Deconstructing Method

One critical question remains: In describing and characterizing deconstruction in the abstract as a double science that is designed to intervene in the binary oppositions that organize both language and logic, haven't we done precisely what Derrida tells us we should not do? Haven't we turned deconstruction into a kind of method? The answer to this question is (and cannot help but be) an undecidable "yes and no."[47] And this is where we need to return to what had been postponed at the very beginning of this chapter: the identification of deconstruction as a "general strategy."

The word "strategy" is of Greek origin and initially was utilized in the context of military operations, specifically naming a calculated plan of attack that then organizes and governs specific actions, or tactics. This sounds suspiciously like a *method*, which, as we have seen previously, can be characterized as a predefined road or pathway to the achievement of some objective. But Derrida immediately complicates things through the addition of the word "general," which is borrowed and derived from Georges Bataille's work with a concept he called "general economy." "The strategy of deconstruction," Scott Cutler Shershow explains, "is called 'general' to acknowledge its link to Bataille's 'general economy': an economy of loss and excess which is opposed to a 'restricted economy' of investment and profit, and intended, above all, to displace the philosophic privilege of the Hegelian 'speculative' dialectic."[48]

As a general strategy, deconstruction is a procedure or protocol that can be pursued and followed, but unlike a method or methodology cannot be restricted or regulated such that one's investment in the process (whether that be time or effort or something else) can be assured of producing predictable and profitable outcomes. Unlike a standard investigative method, in which the researcher generally knows where they are going and how they are going to get there, deconstruction is more adventurous, often producing unexpected, surprising, and even disturbing results. Consequently, "general strategy" is a way to say deconstruction dissimulates something like a method that is, strictly speaking, not a method in the usual sense of the word.

But does that mean that deconstruction is ultimately ambivalent and that Derrida wants to have it both ways—to challenge the hegemony of existing metaphysical concepts and yet continue to use these concepts to name something different? The answer to this question is complicated, but for good reasons. In order for deconstruction to address itself to that which escapes the event horizon of binary opposition, and in order for us to be able to say anything about it that is coherent and understandable, one cannot help but reuse the available language and logic. In other words (as if there ever really were "other words"), if structuralism is right and language, any language, consists in a system of differences, then any possible alternative that would be different and determined to exceed the grasp of binary opposition (or, if you prefer, the law of noncontradiction) can only be described in and by using a vocabulary that is necessarily composed of and contained by binary opposition. In this inescapably difficult situation, language itself comes to be twisted and contorted in such a way as to make that which is fundamentally oppositional in its structure (or, what amounts to the same, governed by the law of noncontradiction) address itself to and articulate that which no longer can be and never was able to be comprehended by such arrangements. This is why Derrida insists on "bifurcated writing," whereby the existing terms are taken up and redeployed against themselves, or a "double play, marked in certain decisive places by an erasure which allows what it obliterates to be read."[49]

At the same time, we need to recognize and be prepared to deal with the fact that these efforts cannot help but run the risk of being reabsorbed and misunderstood according to the established systems of both language and logic. As Derrida explains (and we will give this issue more direct attention in the final chapter): "the hierarchy of dual oppositions always reestablished itself."[50] In the same way that "deconstruction" is always exposed to being reappropriated into the constructionist/destructionist schema by being misunderstood and misconstrued as just another name for what is called "destruction"; so too does the "general strategy" of deconstruction—what we have schematically characterized in this chapter as involving a two-step procedure or double gesture—always and necessarily risk being misidentified and misinterpreted as a method. Consequently, if one insists on calling and understanding deconstruction as a method, this can and will only succeed to the extent that it also and from the very beginning deconstructs method. What this involves and how it actually works is something that will be taken up and developed in chapter 4.

FOR INSTANCE

The preceding chapter provides what is arguably a general and schematic characterization of the double science that is deconstruction. We now turn attention to specific *examples* where deconstruction has taken place or is taking place. But prior to getting into it, we need to take note of two preliminary items.

First, "example" is already the wrong word and, if not sufficiently qualified, a significant obstacle to understanding. The term is typically used to identify a specific instance of a more general or abstract formulation. There is, for instance, the general idea or form of a couch, and then there are specific couches that in one way or another exemplify the concept or idea. This way of thinking, which is common and so widespread as to be considered virtually beyond question, is informed by Platonic philosophy, which distinguished the general form or idea of something from its specific individual instances. But this difference—this distinction between general form and specific instantiations—is THE metaphysical opposition par excellence and therefore is the subject of (or subjected to) deconstruction. What follows, then, are not examples *of* deconstruction (which would conform to the terms of the Platonic formalization, leaving this conceptual duality in place and unquestioned) but examples *in* deconstruction. I know the difference here is small, a matter of prepositions—*of* vs. *in*—but that difference (as we shall see in the course of what follows) makes all the difference.

Second, we will consider two varieties or kinds of examples. In the first place, we will look at one instance where there has been extensive documentation, specifically the speech/writing dichotomy that had initially concerned Derrida and obsessed an entire generation of students and researchers working in the wake of his influence. We will also consider contexts and circumstances where deconstruction has a place (or should have place) but has not yet been fully developed or documented. In fact, we will give precedence to the latter and for good reasons. Retelling or even reproducing the deconstruction of logocentrism (the speech/writing conceptual opposition) for which Derrida is famous would provide little by way of new information or insight. Doing so not only risks replaying what others have presented in greater detail but might leave one with the mistaken impression that deconstruction is something belonging to the not-too-distant past and that its importance is primarily historical. Looking at examples or instances where deconstruction has a place but is not yet fully documented or articulated opens up the effort to the opportunities and challenges of the twenty-first century, bringing deconstruction, as Michael Naas describes it, "closer to home."[1]

Writing

You are reading a book and the words on the page (whether that page is paper or the screen of a digital device) are typically understood as the expression of an author who has something to say. This is because the written word is generally taken to be the representation of what was or would have been spoken, and spoken words are understood to be the direct product or expressions (literally, "pressing out") of mental states, ideas, or thoughts. This way of thinking—a way of thinking not just about thinking but about language and human communication—is old, very old. It goes back at least to Aristotle's *De interpretatione* (On interpretation): "Spoken words are the symbols of mental experience and written words are the symbols of spoken words. Just as all human beings have not the same writing, so all human beings have not the same speech sounds, but the mental experiences, which these directly symbolize, are the same for all, as also are those things of which our experiences are the images."[2]

The assumed primacy of the spoken word has a long tradition in Western thought and comprises what Derrida has identified with and sought to investigate under the term "logocentrism."[3] "If for Aristotle," Derrida writes in *Of Grammatology*, "spoken words (*ta en te phone*) are the symbols of mental experience (*pathemata tes psyches*) and written words are the symbols of spoken words, it is because the voice, producer of the first symbols, has a relationship of essential and immediate proximity with the mind. Producer of the first signifier, it is not just a simple signifier among others. It signifies 'mental experiences' which themselves reflect or mirror things by natural resemblance."[4] According to Derrida's groundbreaking work in this area, logocentrism pervades Western thinking and can be documented as far back as Plato, if not before.

Take for example, the *Phaedrus*, a dialogue that is especially important to Derrida's own writing about this matter. The book in fact begins with a book that Phaedrus has carefully concealed under his cloak.[5] This is, for better or worse, the point of origin for one of the oldest philosophical jokes told in graduate seminars: "Hey, Phaedrus. Is that a book I see hidden beneath your cloak? Or are you just happy to see me?" The book in question is the transcript of a speech recently delivered by the well-known orator Lysias, and Socrates, who was not able to attend its "live" performance (a concept that the *Phaedrus* can be credited with introducing and developing in the first place), is anxious not only to hear an account of what transpired during the performance, but also to have access to the actual discourse as recorded in writing and reproduced through the act of reading.

At the beginning of the *Phaedrus*, therefore, writing is situated as a means for recording speech and reproducing it at a future time and in a place other than that of its original delivery. It is, in other words, conceptualized as a way of capturing and storing spoken discourse so that it can be made present again. This particular understanding is eventually theorized at the dialogue's end, where Socrates and Phaedrus explicitly take up and investigate the art or τέχνη (techné) of writing. The examination begins with Socrates famously recounting a legend he has heard concerning two Egyptian gods, Theuth the inventor of writing and Thamus the king, and concludes with what is now a rather famous indictment of the written word that has, as Derrida and others have documented, been constitutive of the Western tradition. For now, we only need to recall three important highlights:

1. *Writing Is a Technology*—In the account provided in the *Phaedrus*, writing is called τέχνη. This word, which is usually translated as "art" and denotes "a system or method of making or doing," is the etymological

root of our word "technology." Technically speaking, writing is a technology, and the *Phaedrus* arguably is the first recorded debate to address what is now called the philosophy of technology. Unlike speech, which is considered to be a natural and inherent capability of the human species, writing is artificial, external, and technical. As Walter Ong explained in the book *Orality and Literacy*: "Writing (and especially alphabetic writing) is a technology, calling for the use of tools and other equipment: styli or brushes or pens, carefully prepared surfaces, such as paper, animal skins, strips of wood, as well as inks and paints, and much more. . . . By contrast with natural, oral speech, writing is completely artificial."[6]

2. *Writing Is Secondary*—This seemingly natural order of things[7] arranges and justifies what is an unequal hierarchy and axiology (a theory of value with both ethical and aesthetic dimensions) that determines the status and significance of writing and subsequent forms of recording technology and media.[8] Already in the *Phaedrus*, the live performance or event, namely the speech that had been delivered by Lysias, is considered first in both temporal sequence and status. Within the timeframe of the text, the speech of Lysias occurs first; in fact, it has already transpired outside and before the beginning of the dialogue. The record of this speech, the

book with which Phaedrus initially entices Socrates, is introduced and initially positioned as a copy of this original performance. It is, therefore, both secondary and derived. It is a kind of surrogate and proxy of this primary or more original event that takes place by standing in and taking the place of what has passed away and is no longer present. It is a mode of representation.

Compared to the original spoken performance, then, the written record is always somewhat deficient and lacking. It is, as described in the Platonic text, a "mere image" of "the living breathing word" akin to what a painting is in comparison to the actual thing that it depicts.[9] Consequently, the difference between speech and writing is ultimately a matter of life and death. Speech, Plato has Socrates say, is alive insofar as it is animated by the breath of a living speaker; while writing, which utilizes artificial and external apparatus, is dead and lifeless.[10] Or, as Derrida neatly summarizes it with reference to the mythical story of Theuth and Thamus, "The god of writing must also be the god of death. . . . [Writing] substitutes the breathless sign for the living voice."[11]

3. *Logocentrism Is Prototypical*—The speech/writing opposition is not just one logical distinction among others. It is prototypical. In other words, the reason the speech/writing dichotomy is so important and worthy of

attention is because so many other things are informed, supported, and regulated by it. As Derrida explains: "It is not enough to say that writing is conceived out of this or that series of oppositions. Plato thinks of writing, and tries to comprehend it, to dominate it, on the basis of opposition as such. In order for these contrary values (good/evil, true/false, essence/appearance, inside/outside, etc.) to be in opposition, each of the terms must be simply external to the other, which means that one of these oppositions (the opposition between inside and outside) must already be accredited as the matrix of all possible opposition."[12] Writing, Derrida concludes, "far from being governed by these oppositions, opens up their very possibility without letting itself be comprehended by them."[13]

What is demonstrated in the *Phaedrus*, therefore, is not that the speech/writing dichotomy is one binary pair situated alongside others. It is the principle opposition that describes and orders all the other conceptual oppositions that, in one way or another, come to be associated with it. This is why the deconstruction of logocentrism is not something that is of limited interest to individuals involved in literary studies and related disciplines. What makes the deconstruction of logocentrism so important and worth our attention is the fact that it names not just a problem with writing but also is (at least, Derrida argues that it is) the defining condition of the entire Western episteme. What is said about writing (or written about speaking) has important consequences that influence and affect everything.

Derrida takes aim at and deconstructs this influential but often unquestioned order. He does so not because it has somehow ceased to function, or because he is (or has been charged with or misidentified as) some kind of philosophical anarchist who just likes to shake things up for the sake of making trouble. He does so because the speech/writing conceptual opposition arranges an entire way of thinking—what Heidegger calls "metaphysics" and Derrida names "logocentrism"—that organizes and controls virtually everything but goes largely without saying. It is (to borrow a term from information technology) the operating system of philosophical and scientific thinking, which is running in the background and, for this reason, often is taken for granted and not identified as such. To make matters worse (or more interesting), even if and when this logic—this way of thinking and speaking—is able to be identified and questioned, the method of questioning—the very means by which the questions come to be formulated—proceeds in accordance with this very way of thinking, because to do otherwise would be to risk logical consistency and the possibility of coherent communication.

For Derrida, the deconstruction of this pervasive and seemingly inescapable logocentric tradition transpires by way of the double gesture of *overturning* and *displacement*. Overturning involves flipping the script on the standard conceptual opposition, putting deliberate emphasis on the deprecated term "writing" over and against the customarily privileged term "speech." This inversion—like all overturnings and revolutionary interventions—is unavoidably disturbing. And the impact of the disturbance can be gauged by considering how this operation has generated vehement opposition and immediate knee-jerk dismissals from individuals who mistakenly concluded that it must be the assertion of some anthropological fact. As René Wellek protested, Derrida "propounds the preposterous theory that writing precedes speaking, a claim refuted by every child and by the thousand spoken languages that have no written records."[14] This rather ham-fisted conclusion is only possible if, as Derrida has argued in direct response to Wellek (and many others who have followed his misleading lead), one does not fully appreciate or understand the *double* gesture of deconstruction.[15]

This is why deconstruction does not stop at nor can it be satisfied with the first phase of mere reversal or simple inversion. There is always a second phase, namely the eruptive emergence of what Derrida calls a "new concept" that is not able to be contained within or regulated by the existing system of binary oppositions. Now here is where things get complicated, because the new concept that emerges from the deconstruction of the logocentric opposition of speech/writing is called "writing" or better, "arche-writing." This term designates another concept of writing that is prior to and outside of the conventional or vulgar concept of writing that has been defined and characterized in opposition to speech. And here we need to take note of two important items:

1. *Nominal Repetition*—This reuse or recycling of the term "writing" (an operation that Derrida calls *paleonymy* and that we will further investigate in the chapter that follows) certainly does make things confusing, and Derrida is well aware of it: "To leave to this new concept the old name of writing is tantamount to maintaining the structure of the *graft,* the transition and indispensable adherence to an effective *intervention* in the constituted historical field. It is to give everything at stake in the operations of deconstruction the chance and the force, the power of *communication*."[16] Using an old name to designating a new concept—a third term that exceeds the conceptual order from which it had been derived and in which it intervenes—is strategically necessary to be able to say anything at all about deconstruction and its impact. Deconstruction cannot come to speech, be spoken about, or appear in writing, without redeploying and remixing the available set of words and concepts. At the same time that it provides the opportunity of and for communication, however, this paleonymy also

exposes deconstruction to the possibility—a very good possibility—for misunderstanding.

2. *Conceptual Priority*—The priority of (this other concept of) *writing* is conceptual and not a matter of chronology. As Derrida explains: "To speak of a primary writing here does not amount to affirming a chronological priority of fact."[17] But the fact that it is called "writing" certainly complicates things. It explains, for instance, how one could, if one took things out of context or read these statements inattentively, assert the (mistaken) conclusion that Derrida propounds the preposterous theory of the priority of writing or the mere reversal of the hierarchy of speech over writing. But this is explicitly and quite literally not the case. The new concept of writing—this *arche-writing* or what Derrida also calls "a general writing"[18]—is prior not to speech (which would have been the outcome of a simple inversion of the hierarchical order) but to the very conceptual distinction that institutes and regulates the difference between speech and writing in the first place.

We can see how this all comes to pass by returning to the *Phaedrus*. As we have seen, the *Phaedrus* famously differentiates the natural capacity for speech from the technical artifice of writing. This differentiation is anchored in the mythical debate between Theuth and Thamus and

Deconstruction
cannot come to speech,
be spoken about, or
appear in writing,
without redeploying
and remixing the
available set of words
and concepts.

then further developed in the course of the discussion that follows. According to this way of thinking, writing is situated as a rather poor imitation of speech and exposed to all kinds of problems. In fact Plato's Socrates is pretty harsh in his final assessment of the essential deficiencies of the written word:

> Writing has this strange quality, and is very like painting; for the creatures of painting stand like living beings, but if one asks them a question, they preserve a solemn silence. And so it is with written words; you might think they spoke as if they had intelligence, but if you question them, wishing to know about their sayings, they always say only one and the same thing. And every word, when once it is written, is bandied about alike among those who understand and those who have no interest in it, and it knows not to whom to speak or not to speak; when ill-treated or unjustly reviled it always needs its father to help it; for it has no power to protect itself.[19]

Writing on this account is an impotent representation of speech that is essentially out of control and unable to explain what it really means. Socrates follows this indictment by posing an additional question designed to assist the explanation by way of counter-distinction: "Is there not another kind of word, which shows itself to be the legitimate brother of this bastard one, both in the manner of its begetting and in its better and more powerful nature?" Phaedrus answers this question with a question: "What is this word and how is it begotten, as you say?" To which Socrates surprisingly responds with the word "writing"— "The word which is written with intelligence in the mind of the learner, which is able to defend itself and knows to whom it should speak, and before whom to be silent."[20]

This response is both disorienting and disruptive, precisely because the difference between speech and writing is now explained and justified in terms of *writing*. There is, according to the letter of the Platonic text, a more original concept of writing that precedes and has precedence over the speech/writing opposition. This third term—this *arche-writing*—is not something that is inserted into the Platonic text from the outside. It is not smuggled in or purposefully released as a kind of textual virus that is designed to infect the smooth functioning of Platonic language and logic. Instead it is something that emerges from within the field of the Platonic corpus. This is why, as Derrida explains, "the incision of deconstruction, which is not a voluntary decision or an absolute beginning, does not take place just anywhere, or in an absolute elsewhere. . . . It can be made only according to lines of force and forces of ruptures that are localizable in the discourse to be deconstructed."[21] It is for this reason that efforts to call out, criticize, or denounce Derrida for the deconstruction of logocentrism (or even to credit him with it as a kind of accomplishment) amount to little more than a futile exercise in blaming (or crediting) the messenger.

Virtual

Because the conceptual opposition differentiating speech from writing is prototypical, the deconstruction of logocentrism has repercussions affecting the other terminological pairs. One of these, from at least the time of Plato forward, is that which distinguishes *being* from *appearances*. This fundamental difference (what philosophers call "ontological difference") organizes an entire network of logical distinctions that have been definitive and influential: real/illusory, true/false, actual/apparent, genuine/fake, authentic/inauthentic, and so on. And like all metaphysical binary oppositions, these terms have never been on equal footing; the first term of each pair (i.e., real, true, actual, genuine, authentic) has been the privileged term. We already know this and operate according to its structure, even if we have never read a word of Plato. We value and seek what is true, while trying to avoid falsity, deception, and the merely apparent. We want the real thing as opposed to what is artificial, fake, or inauthentic. We seek out the original and dismiss copies as mere reproductions, representations, or counterfeits. Doubt it? Why then are real flowers considered to be better than the artificial, plastic variety? Why does a popular soft drink identify its brand with the trademark "the real thing?" Why does a frozen dessert made with real fruit trump that with artificial flavors and colors?

If you know your Plato, all of this is explained and organized at the center of the *Republic*, in a little parable that is called "The Allegory of the Cave." This remarkable story—something that most high school students have to read—concerns an underground cavern inhabited by men who are confined to sit before a large wall on which are projected shadow images. The cave dwellers are chained in place from childhood and are unable to see anything other than these artificial projections. Consequently, they operate as if everything that appears before them on the wall is, in fact, real and true. They bestow names on the different shadows that pass before their eyes, devise clever methods to predict their sequence and behavior, and even hand out awards to each other for demonstrated proficiency in knowing such things.[22]

At a crucial turning point in the story, one of the captives is released and shown the actual source of the shadows—small puppets paraded in front of a fire light. Although looking directly at the source of the illumination is initially painful and disorienting, the prisoner eventually comes to understand "that what he had seen before was all a cheat and an illusion."[23] From here the newly liberated individual is dragged out of the cavern and, once his eyes become accustomed to the intensity of the sunlight, discovers the real things that exist outside the fictional projections encountered in the subterranean cavern. In comparing the two, the former prisoner sides with the true and the real, no matter how uncomfortable or disorienting the experience. And if given a choice, he would, as Socrates explains, choose to endure anything rather than such a life inside the cave. Plato's allegory, therefore, not only stages the conceptual opposition that distinguishes true reality from the merely apparent or illusory but ends with a decision that assigns value to the former over and against the latter.

The decision and value system initially documented in Plato's "The Allegory of the Cave" is something that finds expression, again and again, throughout the history of philosophy.[24] We have neither the time nor the space to cover it all. So let's simply recall two subsequent iterations—one very academic and the other much more popular.

Robert Nozick's *Anarchy, State, and Utopia* famously postulates something called the "experience machine"—a computer-controlled system with electrodes that directly stimulate the user's central nervous system. "Suppose," Nozick writes, "there were an experience machine that would give you any experience you desired. Super-duper neuropsychologists could stimulate your brain so that you would think and feel you were writing a great novel, or making a friend, or reading an interesting book. All the time you would be floating in a tank, with electrodes attached to your brain."[25] Given this set-up, Nozick then asks whether one would make the decision to plug into this machine for life. In response, he argues that most people, if given such an opportunity, would not: "Plugging into an experience machine limits us to a man-made reality, to a world no deeper or more important than that which people can construct. There is no actual contact with any deeper reality, though the experience can be simulated."[26] Like the decision documented in Plato's *Republic*, Nozick affirms the value of true experiences in the real world over illusory and artificial deceptions, no matter how enjoyable or entertaining the latter might appear to be.

A similar decision is deployed and dramatized in *The Matrix*, a popular film and media franchise from the turn of the century. Early in the first film of the series (initially released in 1999), the rebel leader, Morpheus (played by actor Lawrence Fishburne), presents the film's protagonist, Neo (played by Keanu Reeves), with a choice between two mutually exclusive alternatives, represented by a blue and a red pill. Should Neo decide to swallow the blue pill, he will remain within the computer-generated dreamworld of the Matrix (ostensibly a version of Nozick's experience machine) and know nothing of his decision to do so. Should he decide to swallow the red pill, he will initiate a process that is called the "awakening" and eventually come to experience the reality of the true world that exists outside the artificial experience that is created and sustained by the computers of the Matrix. Consequently, what Morpheus presents to Neo in the form of two different pills are the classic antagonisms that comprise and organize things since the time of Plato: truth vs. deception, being vs. appearance, reality vs. artifice, and authenticity vs. inauthenticity. In the face of these two apparently exclusive options—Morpheus's either/or choice being organized and presented in terms of the principle of noncontradiction—Neo makes what many of us take to be the right choice. He decides to swallow the red pill and live in the real and true world.[27]

This way of thinking works, and that's the problem. It works too well. It comprises something like a default setting in our philosophical operating system. And as long as it continues to work without noticeable friction or problems, we have little or no reason to question it or challenge its basic operations. What works works, end of story. But like all binary oppositions, this metaphysical order arranges an unequal hierarchy of unassailable values that are (and cannot help being) an exertion of power. We see this in politics, where the debate between what is "really real" and what can be dismissed as "fake news" determines the fate of nations. We see it in "the culture wars," where religious fundamentalists (no matter what faith tradition) come into conflict with science over basic questions concerning what is or is not real and true. And we see it in media and technology, where video games, MMORPGs, and social media have been criticized for seducing impressionable users with the artifice of computer-generated deceptions and the appearances of social interaction where there really is little or none of that.[28]

Thus there are good reasons to challenge the legacy and logic of this metaphysical order, and its deconstruction is something that is already evident in and operating at the margins of the tradition. In fact, the deconstruction of this philosophical matrix is, as Derrida has demonstrated, already in play within the texture of Plato's own work. But an even better instance—better for us insofar as it may be more accessible and exemplary—can be found in the work of Friedrich Nietzsche.

In a notebook entry from 1870, the young Nietzsche (who was twenty-six at the time) pushed back against the legacy and logic of Platonic thought, indicating that his research program would seek to institute an inversion of the traditional values: "My philosophy an *upside down Platonism*. The further away from true beings, the purer, more beautiful, the better it is. Life in illusion as goal."[29] Where the tradition of Platonic philosophy—and everything that follows from it, insofar as all of philosophy has been described as a footnote to Plato—validates being, truth, and the real, this fragment proclaims the value of the traditionally deprecated terms: appearances, deceptions, and illusions. This effort at reversing Platonism constitutes the initial phase of deconstruction—the overturning of one of the classic binary oppositions of metaphysics.

Nietzsche, however, was not satisfied with mere reversal. He knew that the overturning of a conceptual opposition essentially changes nothing, because it still operates, albeit in an inverted form, on the terrain of and from the system that is supposedly affected. Consequently, Nietzsche was not content to be a mere philosophical revolutionary. He goes one step further by deliberately displacing the very logic that defines Platonic philosophy. That is, he takes an additional step that ruptures the limits of the philosophical game. This is the second phase of deconstruction—the emergence of a new concept that cannot be contained by the existing order of things. This is perhaps most evident in the parable, included in *Twilight of the Idols*, titled "How the 'True World' Finally Became a Fable." This short text, which proceeds in several discrete steps, ends with the following remarkable statement: "The true world—we have abolished. What world has remained? The apparent one perhaps? But no! *With the true world we have also abolished the apparent one*."[30] Here, Nietzsche moves beyond the mere reversal of Platonism, undermining and destabilizing the very distinction between the true world and its apparitional other. What Nietzsche identifies, therefore, is not a simple inversion of the existing metaphysical order, but a deconstruction of what are perhaps the principal binary oppositions that structure the entire field of philosophical thinking. This operation leaves neither truth nor illusion, reality nor appearance, but something other—something beyond and outside of these logical oppositions that organize all possible modes of thinking and, because of this, exceeds the scope of available designations.

If compelled to provide this undecidable outcome with a designation, it may be called "virtual," a term that has been commonly situated as a kind of synonym for the illusory or the opposite of what is determined to be real and true. As Pierre Lévy explains in the book *Cyberculture*: "The word 'virtual' often signifies unreality, 'reality' here implying some material embodiment, a tangible presence."[31] The virtual, however, is otherwise. It names not the opposite of the real but a third alternative that is neither real nor one of its opposites. As explained by Gilles Deleuze (who has been designated "the philosopher of the virtual" by Slavoj Žižek[32]): "We had opposed the virtual and the real: although it could not have been more precise before now, this terminology must be corrected. The virtual is opposed not to the real but to the actual. The virtual is fully real in so far as it is virtual. Exactly what Proust said of states of resonance must be said of the virtual: 'Real without being actual, ideal without being abstract'; and symbolic without being fictional."[33]

Characterized in this fashion, the virtual is not situated as the opposite of the real, but comprises something that exceeds the grasp of the conceptual differences situated between the real and its logical opposites. As Deleuze concludes, "The virtual is not opposed to the real; it possesses a full reality by itself."[34] Derek Stanovsky extends this line of reasoning to the phrase "virtual reality" and, in the process, circles back to where it all began in Plato's *Republic*: "It is not simply that the representations of virtual reality are false (not genuine) like the reflections in a mirror. It is not even analogous to Plato's view of theater, which was to be banned from his *Republic* because of its distortions and misrepresentations of reality. Instead, virtual reality may summon up a whole new reality, existing without reference to an external reality, and requiring its own internal methods of distinguishing true from false, what is genuine or authentic from what is spurious or inauthentic."[35] Consequently and despite initial appearances, the phrase "virtual reality" is not an oxymoron (a concatenation of opposing terms that violate the law of noncontradiction); it is a new concept designed to identify an alternative that exceeds the boundaries of the existing ontological and axiological categories. The virtual, therefore, deconstructs (or, perhaps better stated, is the outcome of a deconstruction of) the difference situated between the real and its conceptual opposites. It constitutes a nondialectical third term that intervenes in the system of metaphysical concepts by which we have typically distinguished the real from what is merely apparent, fictional, or illusory.

Remix

Another set of metaphysical oppositions that organizes and orders things, helping us to make sense of ourselves and our world, is that which divides and differentiates between original and copy, innovative and derived, or unique and reproduced. And as was the case with the deconstruction of the real, these conceptual pairings arrange unequal hierarchies, where the first term of each pair has ontological and axiological privilege and precedence. The original *Mona Lisa*, which hangs on the walls of the Louvre in Paris, is a priceless and unique artwork protected by alarm systems and armed guards. The insurance value of the painting—the highest ever recorded—is currently estimated to be $850 million U.S. dollars. Meanwhile numerous reproductions of the original work are sold in the museum book store for just a few Euros. Likewise, you can book an Elvis impersonator for your next backyard party, and they will entertain you and your guests with an imitation of something that approximates what it might have been like to have seen the actual Elvis Presley in concert. And when you purchase supplies for the event with cash,

Virtual is not situated as the opposite of the real, but comprises something that exceeds the grasp of the conceptual differences situated between the real and its logical opposites.

especially if you pay in large bills, the clerk will carefully examine the piece of paper to ensure that it is a genuine $100 bill and not a counterfeit reproduction.

This very common and seemingly normal way of thinking is something that can also be traced back to Platonic philosophy. But instead of reproducing the original Platonic formulation, let's look at how it comes to be replayed in more contemporary versions, namely remix. The term "remix" generally refers to the practice of recombining preexisting media content—such as popular songs, films, television programs, texts, and web data—in order to fabricate a new work that is arguably greater than the sum of its parts. Although initially popularized with digital audio, made widely available over the Internet, and heard on dance floors across the globe, remix is not something limited to either digital media or popular music. Analog precursors can be found in the turntable practices of Jamaican dub and hip hop and the audio collage efforts of Pierre Schaeffer's *musique concrète*, John Oswald's Plunderphonics, Negativland, and Vicki Bennett, who works under the name People Like Us.

Similar practices have been developed and pursued in almost every area of artistic effort and content creation. There are, for instance, literary remixes, like Seth Grahame-Smith's recombination of Jane Austin's classic novel *Pride and Prejudice* with B-grade zombie pulp fiction; visual remixes, like Shepard Fairey's iconic "Hope" poster from the 2008 U.S. presidential campaign; and data mash-ups, those Web 2.0 implementations and mobile apps that appropriate and combine content from two or more data sources in order to provide users with a value-added application. Because of the seemingly unrestrained proliferation of the practice across all aspects of contemporary culture, William Gibson has identified remix as the "characteristic pivot" of the twenty-first century and documentary filmmaker Kirby Ferguson has argued that "everything is a remix."[36]

Despite or perhaps because of its popularity, critical responses to remix have pulled in two seemingly opposite directions. On one side, there are the utopian plagiarists, what I call "copyleftists," and remix fans and advocates, those individuals and organizations who celebrate remix and other cut-up and collage practices as new and original ways for creating and distributing media content. "The Internet," as explained by Brett Gaylor, director and narrator of the documentary *Rip!: A Remix Manifesto*, "allowed me to connect from my island to the world, to communicate ideas to millions of others. And a media literate generation emerged, able to download the world's culture and transform it into something different. And we called our new language 'remix.' Funny things, political things, new things were all uploaded back to the net. The creative process became more important than the product as consumers were now creators, making the folk art of the future."[37]

On the opposing side, there are the critics. According to this group (which can be called "the copyright," insofar as they typically seek to conserve traditional values regarding intellectual property protections), the sampling and recombining of preexisting material is nothing more than a cheap and easy way of recycling the work of others, perpetrated by what are arguably talentless hacks who really have nothing new to say. Indicative of this opposing view are the comments offered by indie-rock icon and producer Steve Albini, in another documentary on remix, *Copyright Criminals*: "I've made records with a lot of people; probably the most famous would be Nirvana, the Pixies, Jimmy Page and Robert Plant of Led Zeppelin. As a creative tool, like for someone to use a sample of an existing piece of music for their music. I think it's an extraordinarily lazy artistic choice. It is much easier to take something that is already awesome and to play it again with your name on it."[38] According to Albini, and others who share his opinion, the appropriation and reuse of others' work in a remix is simply cheap and lazy. Unlike real creative artists or media producers, they contend, who have talent and put in the hard work to develop original content, those engaged in remix merely appropriate and recycle the work of others. This effort, it is argued, requires no particular talent or genius and amounts to a kind of stealing and violation of intellectual property by what remix critics consider to be copyright criminals. Or, as forcefully asserted by former Black Flag front man Henry Rollins: "You're a fucking thief of music. You're a record player player. You're DJ turntable."[39]

What is interesting about this debate, however, is not necessarily what makes the two sides different. What is remarkable and needs to be deconstructed is what both sides share in order to enter into debate and to occupy these opposing positions in the first place. Despite their many differences, both sides of the conflict value and endeavor to protect the same things: originality, innovation, and the figure of the hardworking and talented artist. One side sees remix as providing new modes of original content creation that require effort and skill on the part of creative artists; the other argues that there is not much originality, innovation, or effort in merely sampling and remixing prerecorded material. Formulated in this way, these two seemingly opposed positions are fueled by and seek to protect the same underlying values and investments—originality, innovation, uniqueness, creativity. Since these values are already operative in and define the scope and configuration of the current debate, they are often deployed and even defended without ever being questioned or submitted to critical examination. They are (borrowing a phrase that is often used in audio production) "buried in the mix."

What is needed, therefore, is a thorough and complete reevaluation of these shared values—not because they have somehow failed to function, but because they function all too well and often exert influence in the absence of questioning or critical reflection. As long as debate about remix continues to be structured according to this axiology, this ancient theory of moral and aesthetic value that goes at least as far back as Plato, little or nothing will change. Each side will continue to pile up new evidence and arguments in support of its positions, but each side's proponents will, insofar as they seek to protect and advance the same basic principles and underlying values, accomplish little more than agreeing against each other. "They leave us," as Andrew Whelan and Katharina Freund describe it, "in a remix-good/remix-bad binary."[40] The objective, therefore, is to intervene in this conceptual opposition and, in the process, do more than simply endorse one side or the other. What is needed is a deconstruction of this entire conceptual apparatus.

Consider, for example, a specific instance of remix, such as Mark Vilder's (aka Go Home Productions) "Ray of Gob." This audio mashup, which recombines music taken from the Sex Pistol's iconic punk anthem "God Save the Queen" and the lyrical content and vocal performance derived from Madonna's "Ray of Light," is not just a random or haphazard concatenation of different things. It is a deliberate and calculated form of pop-culture blasphemy that not only combines the lyrical content and melody of the original recordings but also preserves the exact sound and unique inflections of both the Sex Pistols' guitar-oriented music and Madonna's recognizable vocal delivery. Vidler's remixed composition, then, does not just sound like Madonna singing to something that sounds similar to the Sex Pistols; it is Madonna actually singing to the musical accompaniment of the Sex Pistols, even though this collaboration as such never actually took place. Consequently, the "Ray of Gob" recording is not the faithful reproduction or documentary record of some original and unique musical performance. It simulates a performance that did not, strictly speaking, ever take place as such.

Remix, therefore, stages (or names the occasion of) a deconstruction of the standard conceptual opposition differentiating the original work from derived copies by way of a double gesture that sides with the depreciated term (copy) and makes available a new concept (remix) that is neither original nor a copy, but copies of copies that produce a new derived original. Remix, we can say, following Deleuze's characterization of *simulation*, "swallows up or destroys every ground which would function as an instance responsible for the difference between the original and the derived."[41] Consequently, the significance of remix consists in neither fidelity to a pristine original nor its mere opposite. It is just as much opposed to faithful representation of an original concept of originality as it is to promiscuous infidelities and merely fooling around.

Deconstruction is not and has never been a form of anything goes.

What this means for remix as both a theoretical concept and cultural practice is the following: Instead of being evaluated on the basis of its innovative originality, which is an argument that has been made time and again by advocates of remix, or on the basis of its diminished status as a mere plagiarized copy of a copy, which is the argument most often mobilized by its detractors, remix succeeds to the extent that it can reverse and displace what would have been mere copies into simulacra that blaspheme this entire conceptual order. A particular remix, like "Ray of Gob," is good to the extent that it is able to release a deconstruction of existing configurations of cultural hegemony in music, visual art, literature, and so on. And the fact of the matter is, some examples of remix do this better than others. All remix is not created equal. Consequently, what makes a remix good is something that needs to be decided on the basis of the particular kind of conceptual interventions it deploys within the material of contemporary culture and the extent to which it makes these interventions perceptible. In some cases, a remix might just make you want to dance, and there is nothing wrong with dancing. In other cases, however, and even at the same time, it potentially violates every aspect of the way we have traditionally made sense of things, causing nothing less than monstrous but incredibly illuminating transgression of existing systems of axiological power.

Cyborg

If we were truly being faithful to Derrida (and clearly, we are not, and that is something he would have probably endorsed anyway), we would need to point out that *blasphemy*, though a very useful concept in these particular contexts, is not one of Derrida's words. It comes from Donna Haraway, specifically her celebrated "socialist feminist" call-to-arms, "A Cyborg Manifesto." Like Derrida, Haraway was deeply concerned by the oppressive hegemony of conceptual oppositions, or the "troubling dualisms" that, as she describes, "have been systemic to the logics and practices of domination of women, people of color, nature, workers, animals—in short, domination of all constituted as others, whose task it is to mirror the self."[42] For Haraway, the figure of the cyborg constitutes a monstrous intervention in and a deconstruction of this tradition, which points the way out of these systems of domination and oppression. "Cyborg imagery," she argues, "can suggest a way out of the maze of dualisms in which we have explained our bodies and our tools to ourselves."[43]

The neologism *cyborg*, which is formed by mashing up the words "cybernetic" and "organism," is not original to Haraway's text. It came from outer space, specifically an article about human space flight written by Manfred Clynes and Nathan Kline and published in the September 1960 edition of *Astronautics*, one of the leading scientific journals of the space age. In this essay, titled "Cyborgs and Space," Clynes and Kline advanced a rather innovative proposal. Because human beings are not capable of surviving in the vacuum of space, astronauts need to be enclosed in a sealed capsule that contains everything necessary to sustain life (i.e. oxygen, water, food, heat, etc.). All of this not only adds weight to the launch vehicle but is, according to Clynes and Kline, fragile and dangerously unsustainable. As an alternative solution to this fundamental problem, they argue that "altering man's [sic] bodily functions to meet the requirements of extraterrestrial environments would be more logical than providing an earthy environment for him in space."[44]

Within the course of this proposal, the duo suggested the word "cyborg" to name this kind of corporeal augmentation, or as they described it, "for the exogenously extended organizational complex functioning as an integrated homeostatic system unconsciously, we propose the term cyborg."[45] Since the time of this initial formulation the word has come to be employed more generally to name any form of integrated synthesis of organism and technology into a hybrid, homeostatic system. And it has been imaginatively visualized in science fiction with the apocalyptic figures of the Terminator, Robocop, and the Borg of *Star Trek*. In fact, the standard image of the cyborg that is familiar to most people is that of a dehumanized monster and the terrifying symptom of a future gone very wrong.

Haraway strategically reappropriates, remixes, and repurposes the concept. And she does so as a deliberately provocation to the dominant modes of late-twentieth-century feminism. The critical target of Haraway's manifesto are the "American radical feminists like Susan Griffin, Audre Lorde, and Adrienne Rich" who, according to Haraway's diagnosis, have "restricted too much" what is possible to say and to think. "They insist on the organic, opposing it to the technological. But their symbol systems and the related positions of ecofeminism and feminist paganism, replete with organicisms, can only be understood in Sandoval's terms as oppositional ideologies fitting the late twentieth century."[46] Haraway does not oppose these thinkers/activists or their efforts at sociopolitical liberation, but seeks to deconstruct the ideologies they patronize and promote. And this is operationalized by way of a double gesture. It begins by deliberately overturning the organic/technological dichotomy, siding with what would be the deprecated term in the eyes of Haraway's ecofeminist colleagues. This revolutionary operation, though a necessary first step, is not sufficient. It is, therefore, supplemented by the emergence of a new concept, cyborg, a monstrous figure that does not fit the existing categorical distinctions.

This is because "cyborg," as Haraway takes up and operationalizes the term, names not just the cybernetic organism that Clynes and Kline had initially envisioned in 1960, but designates a fundamental transformation in the human subject and human subjectivity. "By the late twentieth century," Haraway explains, "we are all chimeras, theorized and fabricated hybrids of machine and organism; in short we are cyborgs."[47] This cyborg assimilation, however, has little or nothing to do with technical augmentation or even metaphoric forms of technological dependency. Instead, "cyborg" names the product of a dual boundary breakdown in existing ontological categories: 1) that between animals (or other organisms) and humans, and 2) that between self-controlled, self-governing machines and organisms, especially humans. And these boundary breakdowns are, as Haraway illustrates, particularly evident in contemporary culture:

> By the late twentieth century in United States, scientific culture, the boundary between human and animal is thoroughly breached. The last beachheads of uniqueness have been polluted, if not turned into amusement parks—language, tool use, social behavior, mental events. Nothing really convincingly settles the separation of human and animal. . . .

Late twentieth century machines have made thoroughly ambiguous the difference between natural and artificial, mind and body, self-developing and externally designed, and many other distinctions that used to apply to organisms and machines. Our machines are disturbingly lively, and we ourselves frighteningly inert.[48]

But Haraway, it is important to point out, does not encourage, produce, or invent these boundary breakdowns. She simply traces the contours and consequences of border skirmishes or untenable discontinuities that have been underway within and constitutive of intellectual history. The cyborg, therefore, does not cause or produce this ontological erosion of the human subject; it merely provides this dissolution with a name. For this reason, "cyborg" identifies not just an enhanced human being, as is formulated in the transhumanist movement. It also describes the rather unstable ontological position in which the human subject already finds itself. Therefore, we can say, performing something of a remix on Bruno Latour, that we have never really been human. We have always and already been cyborg, insofar as the difference between human and animal and animal and machine have been and continue to be undecidable, contentious, and provisional. Consequently, the cyborg threat that is imaginatively visualized with the Borg of *Star Trek* is not some possible future coming at us from deep space; it is a description of the present, if not a characterization of human history in general. It is for this reason that, as the Borg proclaim, "resistance is futile."

The cyborg, then, is neither the dystopian figure of dehumanization popularized in science fiction nor the utopian promise for human improvement and perfection that has been promoted in transhumanism. Instead, it comprises a posthuman figure resulting from the deconstruction of the human. This effort is not a mere theoretical exercise for ivory-tower navel contemplation; it has very real and practical consequences. Despite what one might initially think, the term "human" is not some eternal, universal, and immutable Platonic idea. In fact, who is and who is not human is something that has been open to ideological negotiations and social pressures. At different times, membership criteria for inclusion in club have been defined in such a way as to not only marginalize but also justify the exclusion of others—barbarians, women, Jews, people of color, indigenous communities, and so on. This "sliding scale of humanity"[49] institutes a metaphysical concept of the human that is inconsistent, incoherent, and capricious. It is precisely for this reason that Haraway introduces the cyborg as a blasphemous and monstrous figure that can intervene in and even avoid contributing to the logic and legacy of these violent forms of exclusion, marginalization, and domination. "Perhaps," as Haraway

The cyborg is neither
opposed to nor
an elaboration of the
human but provides
a way to think
outside the box of the
phallogocentric
tradition of humanism.

recommends, "we can learn from our fusion with animals and machines how not to be Man, the embodiment of Western Logos."[50]

Understood in this fashion, the cyborg is neither opposed to nor an elaboration of the human but provides a way to think outside the box of the phallogocentric tradition of humanism, which is not some naturally occurring objective idea but an ideology that promotes and protects certain interests and investments. Consequently, this posthuman subject, as N. Katherine Hayles accurately characterizes it, "does not really mean the end of humanity. It signals instead the end of a certain conception of the human, a conception that may have applied, at best, to that fraction of humanity who had the wealth, power, and leisure to conceptualize themselves as autonomous beings exercising their will through individual agency and choice."[51] In deconstructing both the human and the ideology of humanism, the cyborg provides a way to think otherwise, responding to and taking responsibility for previously marginalized others and other forms of otherness.

CONSEQUENCES AND RISKS

Each of the examples in deconstruction that we have considered is specific and takes place in ways that differ. Despite these differences, there are important similarities
and connections that all four demonstrate and put into
action. In particular, they all take place and can be described in terms of the double gesture that Derrida schematically formulated. Each targets and intervenes in one
of the reigning conceptual oppositions that organize and
order existing systems of knowing: (1) the speech/writing
dichotomy that is the defining condition of logocentrism,
(2) the real/appearance opposition that is a fundamental
organizing principle in metaphysics since Plato, (3) the
original/copy distinction that determines so much in the
area of art and human creativity, and (4) the dualities of
human/animal and human/machine by which we (human
beings) have defined ourselves and justified the anthropo-
centric privilege that is definitive of the entire epoch that

is called "the Anthropocene." The deconstruction of these oppositions proceeds by first flipping the script on the existing oppositional pair and then identifying the eruptive emergence of a new concept—*arche-writing*, *virtual*, *remix*, and *cyborg*—that is a product of the domain that is subject to deconstruction but that cannot be contained or controlled by it.

But why? Why bother with this effort? What does it do for us? The value of all of this is that deconstruction, although informed and made possible by an engagement with the past, provides a way forward into possible futures that are not merely beholden to a repetition of what has gone before. The *raison d'être* of deconstruction, then, is that it opens up the opportunity and possibility to think, to speak, and to act otherwise. In other words, it provides a way to identify, to think about, and to say something that is different and to do so in a way that can make a difference. But again, the skeptical reader might ask (and should ask): Why? Why mess with the status quo, when it seems to work just fine? Or to put it more directly: If it ain't broke, why bother trying to fix it?

Fight the Power

This skepticism appears to be entirely reasonable. The principle of noncontradiction and the arrangement of things into conceptual pairs is a fundamental baseline. Operating in terms of this logic is not an option. We do not, for example, decide to speak and think in opposite terms or not, which is obviously just one more binary opposition; we are already situated in languages and systems of thought that are essentially oppositional in their structure and modes of operation. As Aristotle had asserted in *Metaphysics*, the principle of noncontradiction—whether it concerns ontological facts, epistemological limits, or logical expressions—is fundamental and essentially beyond demonstration. Or as Derrida had explained—channeling the Aristotelean principle of noncontradiction without identifying it as such—this all or nothing way of thinking is not voluntary; it is all or nothing: "Every concept that lays claim to any rigor whatsoever implies the alternative of 'all or nothing.' Even if in 'reality' or in 'experience' everyone believes he knows that there is never 'all or nothing,' a concept determines itself only according to 'all or nothing.' It is impossible or illegitimate to form a philosophical concept outside this logic of all or nothing."[1]

Consequently, thinking and speaking in terms of binary opposition makes sense. And it makes sense precisely because it is the very terms and condition of making sense. So what's the problem? The problem, as Derrida (and others who, in one way or another, can also be situated under the umbrella of poststructuralism) has pointed out, is that these logical oppositions are already prejudicial. They are not and have never been neutral determinations of objective fact. They institute difference and this difference always makes a difference—socially, politically, ethically, ideologically. Conceptual oppositions, wherever and however they appear and are formulated, institute and organize unequal hierarchies that are determinations of value and exertions of power.

Take, for example, the seemingly objective binary opposition of mind/body that does so much of the heavy lifting in modern philosophy. The difference is definitive and influential. It institutes an entire axiological system that gives privilege and precedence to the one term over and against the other. This way of thinking that makes the act of thinking more important than physical embodiment has had devastating consequences. It has permitted human beings to dismiss other animals as mindless automatons that can be used and abused without further consideration. It has been used to justify the global expansion of colonial empires and the domination of one group of people (white Europeans) over others (Africans, the Indigenous peoples of the Americas and Australia, etc.). And it has instituted an entire way of thinking that Nietzsche had called "despisers of the body,"[2] which currently finds expression in various forms of body shaming; the systemic marginalization of "other bodies" (i.e., women, people of color, individuals with physical disabilities, and transgender individuals); and the cyberpunk, techno-utopian ideology of escaping the "meat of the body"[3] by way of direct neural interface to the computer matrix as well as actual research efforts at brain-computer interface (BCI), whole brain emulation, and mind upload.[4] The promise of deconstruction is that it provides a potent mechanism for thinking our way out of the maze of troubling oppositional pairs and dualisms, like mind/body, by which we have made sense of ourselves, our world, and others. All of this sounds promising, especially for individuals and communities who have been, for one reason or another, situated on the "wrong side" of these oppositional dualities. But it is not without costs and potential risks.

Site Specific

Deconstruction is site specific. As Derrida explains: "There is no *one* deconstruction. There are only singular movements, more or less idiomatic styles, strategies, effects of deconstruction that are heterogeneous from one place to another, from one (historical, national, cultural, linguistic, even 'individual') situation to another. This heterogeneity is irreducible and taking account of it is essential to every deconstruction."[5] The deconstruction of logocentrism, for instance, had been developed out of and in response to the linguistic and logical exigencies of Western metaphysics. And this particular effort (at least as Derrida deployed

Deconstruction provides a potent mechanism for thinking our way out of the maze of troubling oppositional pairs by which we have made sense of ourselves, our world, and others.

and developed it) takes place by way of an engagement with the canonical texts of the tradition, which it is hard to deny, reads like a who's who list of dead white males: Plato, Rousseau, Hegel, Husserl, Heidegger, Levinas, and so on.

Does this mean, then, that deconstruction is essentially Eurocentric? The answer to this question has to be (and this should, by now, be no surprise) both yes and no, because what deconstruction targets and works to deconstruct is Eurocentrism. Derrida's efforts to intervene in the phallogocentric tradition that has been the defining condition and focal point of European thought is something that takes place and has its place within the confines of these boundaries. It therefore involves what Derrida has characterized as a parasitic activity, what Spivak describes as "critical intimacy" where one "speaks from inside," or what Haraway calls *blasphemy*—a deliberate and calculated response that understands, acknowledges, and continually works within the margins of an established system.[6] It is by occupying the space of the existing logocentric system and drawing on its language, logic, and conceptual resources that one is able to challenge its hegemony and open it up to alternative configurations, eccentricities, and ways of thinking, speaking, and acting otherwise. And Derrida, for his part, was acutely aware of this, carefully documenting the exigencies of this rather delicate procedure. In fact, the fact that Derrida, on the one hand, has been scathingly criticized for being a philosophical anarchist dead set on "destroying the Western tradition" and, on the other hand, has been taken up and celebrated by a generation of postcolonial and feminist scholars, writers, and activists demonstrates the importance and impact of these efforts to deconstruct Eurocentrism.

But because of its inherent specificity, this does not apply to all instances of deconstruction. In other situations and at other times, there have been difficulties and critical complications. A good example of this can be found in Donna Haraway's "A Cyborg Manifesto." In the essay, Haraway famously proclaims "*we* are cyborgs." [7] But who comes to be interpellated by the first-person plural that is the subject of this statement has been the source of some controversy and critical resistance. For Haraway, the new concept of the cyborg offers a compelling alternative to the hegemony and logic of Western humanism, and she situates this posthuman subject in close proximity to postcolonial theory and practice. Evidence of this affiliation is on display throughout her manifesto. Not only is Haraway's cyborg associated with other interventionist figures and subjects in postcolonial feminist theory (i.e., Gloria Anzaldúa's "la mestiza" or Trinh T. Minh-ha's "inappropriate/d other"[8]), but also, as Andrew Ross had pointed out in the course of an interview with Haraway, it is women of color, especially Asian technology workers, who seem to be privileged as cyborgs in her writing.[9]

This is a problem, and Haraway—a first-world white woman—knows it. "My narrative," she explains in response to Ross's comment, "partly ends up further imperializing, say, the Malaysian factory worker. If I were rewriting those sections of the Cyborg Manifesto I'd be much more careful about describing who counts as 'we,' in the statement, 'We are all cyborgs.' I would also be much more careful to point out that those are subject positions for people in certain regions of transnational systems of production that do not easily figure the situation of other people in the system."[10] In other words, the alternative, posthuman subjectivities introduced by way of the cyborg cannot—without risking a kind of neocolonial violence—be applied broadly to cultures and peoples who have, in the customary estimations of Western humanism, never been adequately recognized as fully human in the first place. Consequently, *cyborg* should not be understood as a new, universal category simply replacing that of the human. It is a highly specific and strategic intervention aimed at and situated within the history and ideology of Western humanism.

Relativism

Related to this is the charge of relativism; the verdict that deconstruction is just a form of free play where anything goes and everything ultimately is permitted. Mark Taylor provides an efficient gloss of the perceived problem in his *New York Times* obituary published a few day after Derrida's death: "To his critics, Mr. Derrida appeared to be a pernicious nihilist who threatened the very foundation of Western society and culture. By insisting that truth and absolute value cannot be known with certainty, his detractors argue, he undercut the very possibility of moral judgment. To follow Mr. Derrida, they maintain, is to start down the slippery slope of skepticism and relativism that inevitably leaves us powerless to act responsibly."[11] And this sort of critical dismissal has, once again, been asserted in direct opposition to statements by Derrida that explicitly assert the exact opposite: "From the standpoint of semantics, but also of ethics and politics, 'deconstruction' should never lead either to relativism or to any sort of indeterminism."[12]

The charge of relativism is often explained and justified by reference to one of the most famous (or notorious) statements attributed to Derrida: *il n'y a pas de hors-texte,* or "there is nothing outside the text." This sentence has been typically (mis)read as a kind of antirealist claim, namely that nothing is real or objectively true and everything is just a socially constructed artifact or effect of discourse. And the fact that the specific instances of deconstruction, at least as they had been developed and represented in the work of Derrida, were always situated in terms of the reading of a text or set of texts certainly does not help matters. But this conclusion is entirely misguided and mistaken, as Derrida had explained in the course of his debate with the American philosopher John Searle: "'There is nothing outside the text.' That does not mean that all referents are suspended, denied, or enclosed in a book, as people have claimed, or have been naïve enough to believe and to have accused me of believing. But it does mean that every referent, all reality has the structure of a differential trace, and that one cannot refer to this 'real' except in an interpretive experience."[13]

What Derrida describes here is neither innovative nor unique. It follows the contours of a crucial philosophical turning point described in Plato's *Phaedo*. In this dialogue, which narrates, among other things, the last moments of Socrates's life, the aged philosopher pauses to reflect on where it all began. In recounting the origin of his endeavors, Socrates describes how he initiated his research by trying to follow the example established by his predecessors and sought wisdom in "the investigation of nature."[14] He explains how this undertaking, despite its initial attraction and his best efforts, continually led him astray, how he eventually gave it up altogether, and how he finally decided on an alternative strategy by investigating the truth of things in λόγος (*logos*), a Greek word that means "word" but is typically translated by a number of related terms, including "language," "reason," and "logic." "So I thought,"

Socrates explains, "I must have recourse to *logos* and examine in them the truth of things."[15] Proceeding in this fashion, however, does not mean that Socrates denied the existence of real things or was merely interested in considering these things as they are reflected or represented in discourse. "Now perhaps my metaphor is not quite accurate," Socrates explains, "for I do not grant in the least that he who investigates things in *logos* is looking at them in images any more than he who studies them in the facts of daily life."[16]

What Socrates advocates, therefore, is not something that would be simply opposed to what is often called "empirical" or "objective knowledge." Instead he advocates an epistemology that questions what Briankle Chang, author of *Deconstructing Communication*, calls the "naïve empiricist picture," which assumes that things can be immediately grasped and known outside the concepts, terminology, and logics that always and already frame our way of looking at or talking about them.[17] In other words, Socrates recognizes that the truth of things is not simply given or immediately available to us. What these things are and how we understand what they are is something that is, at least for our purposes, always mediated through some kind of logical process by which they come to be grasped and conceptualized as such, and this process is always and cannot help but be an expression of values and ideology. Instead of taking sides (or being assigned to a side) in the realist vs. antirealist debate, deconstruction focuses on the unquestioned terms and conditions that make this debate possible in the first place. Not to be too glib about it, one could say that deconstruction deconstructs the realist/antirealist debate.

Communications Problem

Phrases like "deconstruction deconstructs" certainly puts a strain on language. As we have seen throughout the course of this investigation, saying anything about deconstruction inevitably struggles against the exigencies of available terminologies and vocabularies. And there are good reasons for this. If binary opposition (or, if one prefers, the principle of noncontradiction) is not optional but part and parcel of the languages we speak, then any effort to intervene in and disrupt the functioning of this conceptual order necessarily confronts the structural limits of language and the possibility of clear and effective communication. This is why, in "How the 'True World' Finally Became a Fable," Nietzsche cannot help but end with what is essentially unnamable, for that which exceeds the grasp of available concepts—that which is neither *being* nor *appearance* and both *being* and *appearance*—is not able to be designated by any of the available words. As soon as we open our mouths to try to identify this third alternative, as soon as we say something like "It is . . ." or "It is called . . . ," we have fallen back into the system of logical oppositions and terminology that we had sought to challenge in the first place. It is, therefore, not possible to say anything about deconstruction without using the very resources of that which is to be deconstructed.

In responding to this necessary and unavoidable problem, language itself comes to be twisted and contorted in such a way as to make that which is essentially oppositional in its basic structure articulate what can no longer and never was able to be comprehended by such an arrangement. The manner by which this perversion of language is accomplished typically entails the use of two related strategies. On the one hand, there are *neologisms*, the fabrication of brand-new words to designate new concepts or possibilities. This is the strategy employed by Haraway. Though she did not invent the word "cyborg," she did resurrect and redefine this space-age neologism in order to name something that exceeds the usual conceptual oppositions and the limited set of available names. It is through the monstrous figure of the cyborg, Haraway argues, that we can deconstruct the existing systems of oppression and domination that have marginalized women, animals, machines, and others.

Derrida is also known for his neologisms, perhaps the most famous/notorious being *différance*, which is a way to think and write difference differently. "I have," Derrida

It is, therefore, not
possible to say anything
about deconstruction
without using the very
resources of that which
is to be deconstructed.

explains, "attempted to distinguish *différance* (whose *a* marks, among other things, its productive and conflictual characteristics) from Hegelian difference, and have done so precisely at the point at which Hegel, in the greater *Logic*, determines difference as contradiction only in order to resolve it, to interiorize it, to lift it up (according to the syllogistic process of speculative dialectics) into the self-presence of an ontotheological or onto-teleological synthesis."[18] For Derrida, the visibly differentiated *différance* designates a different way to think and write of a difference that remains in excess of the Hegelian concept of difference, which was exclusively understood as negation and contradiction. *Différance*, to say it differently, is a way to think and describe another modality of difference that is not beholden to or limited by the principle of noncontradiction.

On the other hand, there is *paleonymy*. Paleonymy is a Derridean neologism fabricated from available Latin components to name the reuse and repurposing of an "old name in order to launch a new concept."[19] Achieving this requires that the term be carefully selected and strategically reconfigured in order to articulate something other than what it was initially designed to convey. It therefore requires what Derrida characterizes in terms of a double gesture: "We proceed: (1) to the extraction of a reduced predicative trait that is held in reserve, limited in a given conceptual structure, *named X*; (2) to the delimitation, the grafting and regulated extension of the extracted predicate, the name X being maintained as a kind of *lever of intervention*, in order to maintain a grasp on the previous organization, which is to be transformed effectively."[20]

Understood in this way, paleonymy is a kind of verbal remix that samples a deep cut from the available linguistic catalogue and then recontextualizes it to generate something that is new, fresh, and unexpected. These "old names" may be archaic words that have almost fallen off the linguistic radar, like Derrida's appropriation and use of the ancient Greek words, χώρα (chora) and φάρμακον (pharmakon). Or they can be common and more popular words that are stuck with a significant difference that makes them slide away from their usual meaning and usage, as Derrida had done with the term "writing" and Deleuze and others deployed through the appropriation and reuse of the word "virtual."

Reappropriation

Because of this inescapable communications problem, the interventions of deconstruction always and necessarily risk becoming reappropriated into and domesticated by the existing systems of logical opposition that they work to undermine and exceed. The peculiarity of a neologism, for example, comes to be domesticated, through the actions of both advocates and critics, by making it conform to existing conceptual structures, often in the face of explicit statements to the contrary. This has, as we have already seen, been the fate of the term "deconstruction." Despite the fact that, as Derrida has explicitly stated on more than one occasion (and we repeat here, once again, as a kind of refrain), "the 'de-' of deconstruction signifies not the demolition of what is constructing itself, but rather what remains to be thought beyond the constructionist or destructionist schema"[21]; the word has been routinely reabsorbed by and understood according to the constructionist/destructionist schema. In this way, the neologism comes to be domesticated and commodified through a misappropriation that makes deconstruction just another name for "criticism," a synonym for "analysis," a new term for "dismantlement," or the mere opposite of "assembly" and "construction."

The strategy of paleonymy is exposed to a similar difficulty and is often easier to domesticate, because it does not take much interpretive effort to make an old name function in the old way. And Derrida was well aware of the risk: "To put the old names to work, or even just to leave them in circulation, will always, of course, involve some risk: the risk of settling down or of regressing into the system that has been, or is in the process of being deconstructed."[22] *Writing*, for example—which for Derrida "*simultaneously* provokes the overturning of the hierarchy speech/writing, and the entire system attached to it, *and* releases the dissonance of a writing within speech, thereby disorganizing the entire inherited order and invading the entire field"[23]—has often been reappropriated into the existing hegemony of logocentrism. Critics like René Wellek, Walter Ong, John Ellis, and many others have taken Derrida to task on the assumption that he simply overturns the speech/writing hierarchy and, in the face of what appears to be overwhelming empirical evidence to the contrary, dares to promote writing to the position of priority. All of this is perpetrated in direct opposition to or in complete ignorance of carefully worded explanations that have been specifically designed to preempt and protect against such misunderstandings.

Consequently, deconstruction, whether employing the strategy of neologism, paleonymy, or some hybrid mixture of the two, always and necessarily runs the risk of having its interventions reappropriated into the field of conceptual oppositions in which and on which they have been designed to work. This exposure to misunderstanding and domestication is not the result of an individual critic who has it in for deconstruction, even if critics have often exploited this situation for their own purposes. Instead, it is a systemic necessity and unavoidable byproduct of logic and language. If the logical exigency of binary opposition is not optional and resistance to it is effectively futile, then any alternative, no matter how well articulated and contextualized, is immediately and unavoidably exposed to the risk of reappropriation. "The hierarchy of dual oppositions," as Derrida concludes, "always reestablishes itself."[24]

Interminable Analysis

Finally and following from this, there neither is nor can be finality. Because deconstruction is always and necessarily exposed to the risk of reappropriation, the work of deconstruction is never complete or able to be finished. It is and must be what Derrida calls "an interminable analysis,"[25] a never-ending engagement that must continually submit its own innovations, movements, and conclusions to further scrutiny. For this reason, deconstruction does not and cannot conform to traditional models of knowledge production and representation. Its investigations do not and cannot supply anything like a definitive answer or conclusive solution, in the usual sense of the words. Instead its different queries, no matter what angle or aspect is pursued, entail an endless reproduction of questioning that becomes increasingly involved with the complexity of its own problematic. Although this is something that clearly cuts against the grain of common sense, it is necessary if the projects of deconstruction are to be at all successful, consistent, and rigorously applied. This conclusion has a number of consequences, which are (not surprisingly) somewhat inconclusive.

First, this particular form of what appears to be endless self-involvement has engendered important ethical questions and political concerns. "The growing self-reflexivity of theory," Taylor writes, "seems to entail an aestheticizing of politics that makes cultural analysis and criticism increasingly irrelevant."[26] In other words, what's the matter with deconstruction is that as it becomes more and more involved in its own questions and problematics, it appears to be increasingly cut off from the real questions and issues that matter. "Instead of engaging the 'real,' theory seems caught in a hall of mirrors from which 'reality' is 'systematically' excluded."[27] This line of criticism (which is related to the charge of relativism that we considered earlier) is nothing new for philosophy or philosophers. Consider the case of Thales as recounted in Plato's *Theaetetus*: "While he was studying the stars and looking upwards, he fell into a pit, and a neat, witty Thracian servant girl jeered at him, they say, because he was so eager to know the things in the sky that he could not see what was there before him at his very feet."[28]

So it is with the critics of deconstruction, who find the very idea of an interminable analysis to be self-involved or solipsistic and a potentially dangerous kind of intellectual distraction that could lead one to miss and completely disregard what is most important and closest at hand. At the same time, however, deconstruction already has a response to the criticism, which, it rightfully points out, necessarily mobilizes and is formulated in terms of the classic logical oppositions that deconstruction had put in question in the first place. So instead of providing an easy excuse for dismissing deconstruction, this criticism betrays the very problem-space of ethics and politics to which deconstruction responds and for which it takes responsibility.

Second, recursive efforts like that of deconstruction often appear to be less than scientific or at least contrary to a concept of science understood and imagined as linear progress that seeks objective knowledge. But this conclusion is not necessarily accurate. Everything depends on how one understands and operationalizes the term "science." In having the configuration of an interminable analysis, deconstruction dissimulates (with at least one crucial difference) the *speculative science* that is the hallmark of Hegel's philosophical sciences. For Hegel, "speculative" was not, as is often the case in colloquial usage, a pejorative term meaning groundless consideration or idle review of something that is inconclusive. Instead, Hegel understood and utilized the term "speculative" in its original and strict etymological sense, which is derived from the Latin noun *speculum*, meaning mirror. Understood in this way, a *speculative science* is a form of self-reflective knowing. That is, it consists in a mode of cognition that makes its own operations and outcomes an object of its consideration.

Like the speculative science that was described by Hegel, deconstruction does not approach and ascertain its object of investigation from the outside but makes itself and its own innovations the subject of investigation.[29] It is, therefore, a thoroughly self-reflective undertaking that continually must submit its own operations and advancements to reevaluation. However, unlike the Hegelian system, which did have a definite teleological orientation and exit strategy, deconstruction seems to be caught in the vortex of what can only appear to be an infinite regress of endless self-reflection and auto-affective inquiry. This is not, despite first appearances, a pointless exercise or an instance of what Hegel had called "a bad or spurious infinite."[30] It is an interminable struggle that occupies the space of thinking and works within its structures to articulate, however tardy and incomplete, what necessarily remains in excess of its grasp.

Third, although this outcome cuts across the grain of the usual set of expectations, it is a necessary and unavoidable aspect of the philosophical enterprise. The prototypical philosopher, Socrates, does not get himself in trouble for proclaiming inconvenient truths or peddling fake news. He gets himself in trouble with his fellow citizens and is eventually put to death for merely asking questions.[31] Since Socrates, philosophers (on both ends of the analytic/continental philosophical divide[32]) have characterized the task of philosophy in similar ways.

"I am," Daniel Dennett explains, "a philosopher, not a scientist, and we philosophers are better at questions than answers. I haven't begun by insulting myself and my discipline, in spite of first appearances. Finding better questions to ask, and breaking old habits and traditions of asking, is a very difficult part of the grand human project of understanding ourselves and our world."[33] Slavoj Žižek provides something similar: "There are not only true or false solutions, there are also false questions. The task of philosophy is not to provide answers or solutions, but to submit to critical analysis the questions themselves, to make us see how the very way we perceive a problem is an obstacle to its solution."[34] Consistent with this effort, deconstruction does not seek to provide definitive answers or solutions to existing problems. It seeks to demonstrate how the very way we conceive of and talk about a problem is already a problem and a potential obstacle to developing a solution.

Final Analysis

In the final analysis we can say that deconstruction is neither a form of critical analysis nor does it seek out, achieve, or have any pretensions to finality. It is and can

Deconstruction does not seek to provide solutions to existing problems. It seeks to demonstrate how the very way we conceive of and talk about a problem is already a problem.

only take place as an endlessly open form of engagement with existing systems of thought in an effort to challenge the status quo and provide potent opportunities to think, speak, and act otherwise. This does not mean, however, that deconstruction is a form of textual free play where anything goes and all things are permitted. Quite the contrary. It proceeds by and necessitates excessive attention to the exigencies of language and logic in order to follow and apprehend every nuance of their intricate operations, procedures, and protocols. And it does so not to repeat what has gone before—even if, at times, it comes close to repetition—but to extract from such effort a difference that opens onto alternative opportunities and challenges that can make a difference.

GLOSSARY

Analysis
The process of breaking apart a composite structure in order to identify and isolate the smaller, constitutive parts that comprise the whole.

Arche-writing
A Derridean neologism that designates another concept of "writing" that is prior to and outside of the conventional or vulgar concept of writing that has been defined and characterized in opposition to speech.

Axiology
The branch or division of philosophy that investigates and contends with the nature of value and value judgments. It is the collective term for ethics and aesthetics.

Blasphemy
A form of calculated and productive irreverence that is not simply opposed to a particular faith tradition but that undermines, from within the enclosure of that that faith tradition, what is considered to be most valuable, sacred, and beyond question.

Critique
A word of Greek origin denoting "to separate," "to discern," or "to cut (apart)." In contemporary usage, the word has two meanings. In its general and colloquial sense, it commonly has a negative connotation, indicating a form of judgmental evaluation or rudimentary fault-finding. In its more specific philosophical sense, especially in the work of Immanuel Kant, the word designates a method of analysis that seeks to identify and expose a particular system's fundamental operations and conditions of possibility, demonstrating how what initially appears to be beyond question and entirely obvious does, in fact, possess a complex history that not only influences what proceeds from it, but also is itself often not recognized as such.

Cyborg
A portmanteau that combines the words "cybernetic" and "organism." It was initially devised to identify an integrated homeostatic system consisting of both artificial and organic components; and later appropriated by Donna Haraway in the essay "A Cyborg Manifesto" to identify the dual boundary breakdown situated between the ontological categories of human/animal and human/machine.

Différance
A Derridean neologism that designates a different way to think and write of a difference that remains in excess of the Hegelian concept of difference, which had been exclusively understood as negation and contradiction. The small difference that distinguishes *différance* from *difference* is something that can only be differentiated in and by writing.

λόγος/Logos
A Greek word that literally means "word" and is typically defined as "language," "speech," "reason," or "logic."

Logocentrism
A way of thinking about thinking and language that gives central importance to the spoken word as the first signifier—"first" in terms of both sequence and status—and thereby differentiating it from writing, which, by comparison to speech, is a secondary and derived representation or image. For Derrida, this way of thinking defines an entire epoch that others have called "(Western) metaphysics."

Metaphysics
The division of philosophy that deals with first principles, including the fundamental nature of reality and being itself.

Metáporo
A neologism developed by Ciro Marcondes Filho to name an investigative procedure that is other than a method. Unlike a standard research method, which describes a predefined path to achieve a particular investigative objective, *metáporo* designates a procedure that is more flexible and responsive to the particular, where the object of the investigation charts its own path and the researcher learns to accompany it without a prescribed route or assurances of a predetermined outcome.

Neologism

A newly fabricated word that is designed to name or designate a new idea, object, or thought content.

Noncontradiction

A fundamental principle in logic, which states that contradictory propositions cannot both be true in the same sense at the same time; i.e., the two propositions "S is P" and "S is not P" are incompatible and mutually exclusive.

Paleonymy

A Derridean neologism that designates the (re)use of old words to name a new idea, concept, or thought content.

Phallogocentrism

A Derridean neologism designed to refer to the often unquestioned masculine privilege in the texts and traditions of logocentric metaphysics.

Poststructuralism

A late-twentieth-century intellectual movement in philosophy, semiotics, and literary theory that sought to think difference differently by devising alternative tactics to subvert the grid of binary oppositions with which it was believed structuralism could capture reality.

Remix

The practice of recombining preexisting media content—popular songs, films, television programs, texts, web data, etc.—in order to fabricate a new work that is arguably greater than the sum of its parts.

Speculative

A word of Latin origin indicating "mirroring" or "reflection." In the *speculative science* of G. W. F. Hegel, the word indicates a form of self-reflective knowing whereby the subject of the investigation is subjected to investigation such that it become the object of contemplation.

Structural linguistics

An approach to linguistics developed in the work of Ferdinand de Saussure and an influential component of structuralism. Saussure's *Course in General Linguistics*, which was assembled from student notes and published posthumously in 1916, advanced the thesis that the fundamental element of language is the sign and the formal structure of the sign is binary opposition or difference.

Structuralism

A twentieth-century intellectual development that was applied in fields as diverse as linguistics, anthropology, literary theory, sociology, and philosophy. Although it does not name a formal discipline or singular method of investigation, its innovations are widely recognized as the result of developments in the structural linguistics of Ferdinand de Saussure.

Τέχνη/Techné

A Greek word that is usually translated as "art" and denotes "a system or method of making or doing." It is the etymological root of the word "technology."

Unheimlich

A word of German origin meaning both "unhomely" and "uncanny." The word has particular significance in the work of Sigmund Freud and Martin Heidegger.

Virtual

An ontological category designating not the opposite of the real but a third alternative that is neither real nor one of its opposites, i.e., unreal, fictional, or illusory.

NOTES

Chapter 1

1. We should note that this is a common problem. In book 11 of the *Confessions*, for instance, St. Augustine begins his examination of the concept of time with the following remark: "What, then, is time? I know well enough what it is, provided that no one asks me; but if I am asked what it is and try to explain, I am baffled." Being baffled is not necessarily a bad thing. It is, as philosophers from Aristotle to Martin Heidegger have confessed, the main reason behind and the motivating force of any kind of thoughtful investigation.

2. Jacques Derrida, "Afterword," in *Limited Inc*, trans. Samuel Weber (Evanston, IL: Northwestern University Press, 1993), 147.

3. This phrase, "father of deconstruction," appears extensively in both popular and academic literature: Mark Goldblatt, "*Derrida*, Derrida, Etc," *National Review*, January 16, 2003, https://www.nationalreview.com/2003/01/derrida -derrida-etc-mark-goldblatt/; Jonathan Kandell, "Jacques Derrida, Abstruse Theorist, Dies at 74," *New York Times*, October 10, 2004, https://www.nytimes .com/2004/10/10/obituaries/jacques-derrida-abstruse-theorist-dies-at-74. html; Hillary Putnam, *Renewing Philosophy* (Cambridge, MA: Harvard University Press, 1992); Vincent B. Leitch, *Literary Criticism in the 21st Century: Theory Renaissance* (New York: Bloomsbury, 2014).

4. Christopher Orlet, "Derrida's Bluff," *The American Spectator*, October 15, 2004, https://spectator.org/49462_derridas-bluff/.

Chapter 2

1. Jacques Derrida, "Letter to a Japanese Friend," trans. David Wood and Andrew Benjamin, in *Psyche: Inventions of the Other*, vol. 2, ed. Peggy Kamuf and Elizabeth G. Rottenberg (Stanford, CA: Stanford University Press, 2008), 1–2.

2. Michel Foucault, "What Is an Author?," trans. Josué V. Harari, in *The Foucault Reader*, ed. Paul Rabinow (New York: Pantheon Books, 1984), 119.

3. Roland Barthes, "Death of the Author," in *Image, Music, Text*, trans. Stephen Heath (New York: Hill & Wang, 1978).

4. For more on this question, see Simon Critchley, *The Ethics of Deconstruction* (Edinburgh: Edinburgh University Press, 2014).

5. The word "appropriate," is, technically speaking, inappropriate. As Derrida had explained in the "Afterword" to *Limited Inc*, trans. Samuel Weber

(Evanston, IL: Northwestern University Press, 1993, 141; italics in original): "Deconstruction in the singular cannot be simply 'appropriated' by anyone or anything. Deconstructions are the movements of what I have called 'expropriation.' Anyone who believe they have appropriated or seen appropriated something like deconstruction in the singular is *a priori* mistaken." This is one of the reasons why the word, here and elsewhere throughout this book, will be written "(mis)appropriate."

6. According to what Spivak has reported, Derrida had initially employed the word "destruction." As she writes in a parenthetical aside contained in the translator's introduction to *Of Grammatology* (Baltimore: Johns Hopkins University Press, 1976, xlix): "It is interesting to note that, in the first published version of *De la grammatologie*, Derrida uses the word 'destruction' in place of 'deconstruction.'"

7. Martin Heidegger, *Being and Time*, trans. John Macquarrie and Edward Robinson (New York: Harper & Row, 1962), 63.

8. Jacques Derrida, "There Is No One Narcissim," trans. Peggy Kamuf, in *Points . . . Interviews, 1974–1994*, ed. Elisabeth Weber (Stanford, CA: Stanford University Press, 1995), 211.

9. Jacques Derrida, "Negotiations," in *Negotiations: Interventions and Interviews, 1971–2001*, ed. and trans. Elizabeth G. Rottenberg (Stanford, CA: Stanford University Press, 2002), 16.

10. Derrida, "Afterword," 147.

11. Derrida, "Letter to a Japanese Friend," 4.

12. J. Hillis Miller, "Critic as Host," in *Deconstruction and Criticism*, ed. Geoffrey H. Hartman (New York: Continuum, 1979), 206.

13. Gayatri Chakravorty Spivak, *In Other Worlds: Essays in Cultural Politics* (New York: Routledge, 1998), 22.

14. Brian Greene, *The Fabric of the Cosmos: Space, Time, and the Texture of Reality* (New York: Vintage Books, 2005); Stephen P. Stich, *Deconstructing the Mind* (Oxford: Oxford University Press, 1998); Erica Burman, *Deconstructing Developmental Psychology* (New York: Routledge, 2016); Gary Thomas and Andrew Loxley, *Deconstructing Special Education and Constructing Inclusion* (New York: Open University Press, 2007).

15. Steve Ettlinger, *Twinkie, Deconstructed* (New York: Hudson Street Press, 2008); Mohammad Rahman, *C# Deconstructed: Discover How C# Works on the .NET Framework* (New York: Apress, 2014); Elissa Meyich, *Rip It! How to Deconstruct and Reconstruct the Clothes of Your Dreams* (New York: Simon & Schuster, 2006); Bridgett Artise and Jen Karetnick, *Born-Again Vintage: 25 Ways to*

Deconstruct, Reinvent, and Recycle Your Wardrobe (New York: Potter Craft, 2008); Alison Gill, "Deconstruction Fashion: The Making of Unfinished, Decomposing and Re-assembled Clothes," *Fashion Theory* 2, no. 1 (1998): 25–49, https://doi.org/10.2752/136270498779754489.

16. Jennifer Roberts, *Redux: Designs that Reuse, Recycle, and Reveal* (Salt Lake City: Gibbs Smith, 2005), 126.

17. Alastair Macaulay, "The Many Faces of 'Black Swan,' Deconstructed," *New York Times*, February 9, 2011, https://www.nytimes.com/2011/02/10/arts/dance/10swan.html; A. O. Scott, "Deconstructing the Realities of Politics and Terrorism," *New York Times*, December 9, 2005, https://www.nytimes.com/2005/12/09/movies/deconstructing-the-realities-of-politics-and-terrorism.html; Nicholas St. Fleur, "A Paleontologist Deconstructs 'Jurassic World,'" *New York Times*, June 12, 2015, https://www.nytimes.com/interactive/2015/06/12/science/jurassic-world-deconstructed-by-paleontologist.html.

18. London Film School, *Deconstructing the Soundtrack: A School of Sound Masterclass*, 2020, https://lfs.org.uk/workshops/lfs-workshops/252/deconstructing-soundtrack-school-sound-seminar-series; Jason Hellerman, "Deconstructing Film Lighting: What Kinds of Sources Do the Pros Use?" *No Film School* (2019), https://nofilmschool.com/Deconstructing-film-lighting; Scott Freiman, *Deconstructing the Beatles*, 2020, http://www.beatleslectures.com/; Lucy Lean, *Made in America: Our Best Chefs Reinvent Comfort Food* (New York: Welcome Books, 2011).

19. Derrida, "Letter to a Japanese Friend," 4.

20. Barbara Johnson, "Translator's Introduction," in Jacques Derrida, *Disseminations* (Chicago: University of Chicago Press, 1981), xv.

21. Derrida, "Letter to a Japanese Friend," 4.

22. Derrida, 4.

23. Rodolphe Gasché, *The Tain of the Mirror: Derrida and the Philosophy of Reflection* (Cambridge, MA: Harvard University Press, 1987), 121.

24. J. Hillis Miller, *For Derrida* (New York: Fordham University Press, 2009), 60.

25. Derrida, "Afterword," 141.

26. Derrida, "Letter to a Japanese Friend," 4.

27. Jacques Derrida, *Memoires for Paul de Man*, trans. Cecile Lindsay, Jonathan Culler, and Eduardo Cadava (New York: Columbia University Press, 1986), 123.

28. Miller, *For Derrida*, 87.

29. Jacques Derrida, "Psyche: Inventions of the Other," trans. Catherine Porter, in *Psyche: Inventions of the Other*, vol. 1, ed. Peggy Kamuf and Elizabeth Rottenberg (Stanford, CA: Stanford University Press, 2007), 23.

30. Ciro Marcondes Filho, *O Rosto e a Máquina: O Fenômeno da Comunicação Visto Pelos Angulos Humano, Medial e Tecnológico. Nova Teoria da Comunicação*, vol. 1 (São Paulo: Paulus, 2013), 58 (translation by the author); italics in original.

31. Derrida, "Letter to a Japanese Friend," 4.

32. Ian Buchanan, *A Dictionary of Critical Theory* (New York: Oxford University Press, 2016), 489. It has been argued that deconstruction, although initially identified and developed in Europe under the name of Derrida, found its proper place and time in the United States during the final three decades of the twentieth century. There was, in fact, an entire set of invited talks, interviews, and publications at this time organized under and marked with the title "Deconstruction in America." As Derrida had explained in interviews from the period (cf. James Creech, Peggy Kamuf, and Jane Todd, "Deconstruction in America: An Interview with Jacques Derrida," *Critical Exchange* [Winter 1985]), deconstruction appears to be an imported concept and something that, although coming from Europe, takes place and has its proper place in America. This geopolitical explanation, however, is not so simple and straightforward, and Derrida complicates the picture at the beginning of a lecture that was dedicated to the memory of Paul de Man and was first delivered, in the United States, shortly after de Man's death: "Can we speak of 'deconstruction in America'? Does it take place in the United States? First in Europe, and then in America—as some too quickly conclude, thereby raising the questions of reception, translation, appropriation, etc.? . . . Contrary to what is so often thought, deconstruction is not exported from Europe to the United States. Deconstruction has several original configurations in this country, which in turn—and there are many signs of this—produce singular effects in Europe and elsewhere in the world" (Derrida, *Memoires for Paul de Man*, 14–15). So even the seemingly simple question concerning the proper place and location of deconstruction—Is it a European import to America that then appears to come back to Europe? Does it first come into its own on American soil? Or is it a distinctly American product and invention?—is something that does not have a simple and direct answer. This is—however accurate, precise, and correct Derrida's characterization—one more symptom or piece of evidence that has permitted critics to tag Derrida with the burdensome judgment of being "abstruse," "obtuse," and "obscurantist."

33. Paul de Man, *Allegories of Reading: Figural Language in Rousseau, Nietzsche, Rilke and Proust* (New Haven, CT: Yale University Press, 1979), 17.

34. Jonathan Culler. *On Deconstruction: Theory and Criticism after Structuralism* (Ithaca, NY: Cornell University Press, 1982), 109.

35. Wlad Godzich, "The Domestication of Derrida," in *The Yale Critics: Deconstruction in America*, ed. Jonathan Arac, Wlad Godzich, and Wallace Martin (Minneapolis: University of Minnesota Press, 1986).

36. Johnson, "Translator's Introduction," xv.

37. Johnson, xv.

38. Geoffrey H. Hartman, "Introduction," in *Deconstruction and Criticism*, ed. Geoffrey H. Hartman (New York: Continuum, 1979), ix. The history of the Yale School—its rise to prominence, its influence both in the academy and beyond, and its eventual demise—is a compelling drama in its own right. For more on this subject, cf. Mark Currie's *The Invention of Deconstruction* (New York: Palgrave Macmillan, 2013) and Marc Redfield's *Theory at Yale: The Strange Case of Deconstruction in America* (New York: Fordham University Press, 2016).

39. Denis Donoghue, "Deconstructing Deconstruction," *New York Review of Books* 27, no. 10 (June 12, 1980), 41, https://www.nybooks.com/articles/1980/06/12/deconstructing-deconstruction/.

40. Colin Campbell, "The Tyranny of the Yale Critics," *New York Times Magazine*, February 9, 1986, section 6, 20, https://www.nytimes.com/1986/02/09/magazine/the-tyranny-of-the-yale-critics.html.

41. Jeffrey T. Nealon, *Double Reading: Postmodernism after Deconstruction* (Ithaca, NY: Cornell University Press, 1993), 28.

42. Nealon, *Double Reading*, 28.

43. Barbara Johnson, *A World of Difference* (Baltimore: Johns Hopkins University Press, 1987), 11.

44. Derrida, for his part, did not simply and directly oppose these mischaracterizations but recognized in even the most negative and harshest of criticisms something that contributed to the work of deconstruction. He explained this during a 1985 interview with James Creech, Peggy Kamuf, and Jane Todd ("Deconstruction in America: An Interview with Derrida," *Critical Inquiry* 17 (1985): 26): "I am persuaded—and I say this without cynicism, because I think that's the way it happens all the time—I am really persuaded that the people you named are doing very good work for deconstruction." Derrida, therefore, interpreted the critical efforts of individuals like Denis Donoghue, René Wellek, John Searle, and others not as something negative to fight against but as an opportunity to advance the cause of deconstruction. "We have," Derrida continues, "enough history behind us to know how things happen in culture. At a given moment, when some motif is in the process of becoming dominant, all the attacks against it only manage to feed the opposing force. That's the way it goes until the moment it all turns back around. But there is always a phase during which dedicated hostility has an inverse effect, in an absolutely

mechanical way. That's the way it has to be. I think, I hope that it's happening that way, and that reactionism is part of the establishing of deconstruction" (26).

45. Crichley, *Ethics of Deconstruction*, 22; italics in original.

46. Derrida, "There Is No One Narcissism," 213.

47. Derrida, 213.

48. Mark Wigley and Philip Johnson, *Deconstructivist Architecture* (New York: Museum of Modern Art, 1998), 17.

49. Michael Naas, *Miracle and Machine: Jacques Derrida and the Two Sources of Religion, Science, and the Media* (New York: Fordham University Press, 2012).

50. The German adjective *unheimlich*, which was an influential concept for both Freud and Heidegger, can be translated as "uncanny" and "unhomely." The uncanny/unhomely aspects of deconstruction's interaction with architecture had been the subject of intense discussion/investigation, beginning with an academic conference called "Das Unheimliche: Philosophy, Architecture, The City" that convened at DePaul University, April 26–27, 1991. Participants in this two-day meeting included philosophers (i.e., Jacques Derrida, David Farrell Krell, Peg Birmingham, John Sallis) and architects (i.e., Daniel Libeskind, Peter Eisenman, Stanley Tigerman, Ben Nicholson, Catherine Ingraham). The proceedings of the event were published in a special issue of the journal *Research in Phenomenology* 22 (1993) titled "Deconstruction and the Architecture of the Uncanny."

51. It should be noted that this phrase—"deconstructing deconstruction"— has been utilized numerous times over the years by both critics and advocates: Donoghue, "Deconstructing Deconstruction"; Marjorie Hewitt Suchocki, "Deconstructing Deconstruction: Language, Process, and a Theology of Nature," *American Journal of Theology & Philosophy* 11, no. 2 (1990): 133–142, https://www.jstor.org/stable/pdf/27943772; Andrew Stables, "Deconstructing Deconstruction," *English in Education* 26, no. 3 (1992): 19–23, https://doi.org/10.1111/j.1754-8845.1992.tb01076.x; Sandra A. Wawrytko, "Deconstructing Deconstruction: Zhuang Zi as Butterfly, Nietzsche as Gadfly," *Philosophy East and West* 58, no. 4 (2008): 524–551, http://www.jstor.org/stable/40213537.

52. Jacques Derrida, *Dissemination*, trans. Barbara Johnson (Chicago: University of Chicago Press), 112.

Chapter 3

1. For some reason, when it comes to this subject matter, people like or cannot avoid using the image of nutshells. As John D. Caputo explains at the beginning

of a book that is titled *Deconstruction in a Nutshell* (New York: Fordham University Press, 1997, 32): "Whenever deconstruction finds a nutshell—a secure axiom or a pithy maxim—the very idea is to crack it open and disturb this tranquility. Indeed, that is a good rule of thumb in deconstruction. That is what deconstruction is all about, its very meaning and mission, if it has any. One might even say that cracking nutshells is what deconstruction is." For another use of the nutshell image—in a short, two-page explainer that is arguably more of a nutshell—see Gary Rolfe, "Deconstruction in a Nutshell," *Nursing Philosophy* 5, no. 3 (2004): 274–276, https://doi.org/10.1111/j.1466-769X.2004.00179.x.

2. Jacques Derrida, *Positions*, trans. Alan Bass (Chicago: University of Chicago Press), 41.

3. Friedrich Nietzsche, *Beyond Good and Evil*, trans. Walter Kaufmann (New York: Vintage Books, 1989), 10.

4. Jacques Derrida, "Limited Inc a b c . . . ," trans. Samuel Weber, in *Limited Inc*, ed. Gerald Graff (Evanston, IL: Northwestern University Press, 1993), 93.

5. Derrida, *Positions*, 19.

6. Barbara Johnson, *A World of Difference* (Baltimore: Johns Hopkins University Press, 1987), 12.

7. Paula Gottlieb, "Aristotle on Non-contradiction," *Stanford Encyclopedia of Philosophy*, 2019, https://plato.stanford.edu/entries/aristotle-noncontradiction/.

8. This intervention, it should be noted, was not situated in and formalized as a response to Aristotelian logic. Had it been, Derrida's contributions may have had a much warmer reception among academic philosophers, who generally dismissed his work out of hand. Perhaps the best indication of this was the open letter published on May 9, 1992, in the *Times of London*, signed by a number of well-known and notable academic philosophers (including David Armstrong, Ruth Barcan Marcus, Willard Van Orman Quine), and offered in opposition to Cambridge University's plan to present Derrida with an honorary degree in philosophy. "In the eyes of philosophers," the letter reads, "and certainly among those working in leading departments of philosophy throughout the world, M. Derrida's work does not meet accepted standards of clarity and rigour." The letter has been reprinted in *Cambridge Review* 113 (October 1992): 138–139; and Jacques Derrida, *Points . . . Interviews, 1974–1994*, ed. Elisabeth Weber (Stanford, CA: Stanford University Press, 1995): 419–421.

9. Jean Baudrillard, *The Intelligence of Evil, or the Lucidity Pact*, trans. Chris Turner (New York: Berg, 2005), 4.

10. Jonathan Culler, *On Deconstruction: Theory and Criticism after Structuralism* (Ithaca, NY: Cornell University Press, 1982), 98–99.

11. Ferdinand de Saussure, *Course in General Linguistics*, trans. Wade Baskin (London: Peter Owen, 1959), 120; italics in original.

12. Jay David Bolter, *Writing Space: The Computer, Hypertext, and the History of Writing* (Hillsdale, NJ: Lawrence Erlbaum and Associates, 1991), 197.

13. Jacques Derrida, *Of Grammatology*, trans. Gayatri Chakravorty Spivak (Baltimore: Johns Hopkins University Press, 1976), 158.

14. Daniel Chandler, *Semiotics: The Basics* (New York: Routledge, 2002), 102.

15. Peter Elbow, "The Uses of Binary Thinking," *Journal of Advanced Composition* 13, no. 1 (1993): 51, http://www.jaconlinejournal.com/archives/vol13.1/elbow-uses.pdf.

16. Aristotle, *The Metaphysics, Bk. I–IX*, trans. by Hugh Tredennick (Cambridge, MA: Harvard University Press, 1980), 1006a, 1–5.

17. Derrida, *Positions*, 41.

18. W. Lawrence Hogue, "Radical Democracy, African American (Male) Subjectivity, and John Edgar Wideman's *Philadelphia Fire*," *Melus* 33, no. 3 (September 2008): 45, https://doi.org/10.1093/melus/33.3.45.

19. Donna J. Haraway, *Simians, Cyborgs, and Women: The Reinvention of Nature* (New York: Routledge, 1991), 177.

20. Hannah Arendt, *Thinking without a Banister: Essays in Understanding 1953–1975* (New York: Schocken Books, 2018), 461.

21. Audre Lorde, "The Master's Tools Will Never Dismantle the Master's House," in *Sister Outsider: Essays and Speeches* (Berkeley, CA: The Crossing Press, 1984), 110.

22. Mark Taylor, *Hiding* (Chicago: University of Chicago Press, 1997), 269.

23. Johnson, *A World of Difference*, 12.

24. Catherine Belsey, *Poststructuralism: A Very Short Introduction* (New York: Oxford University Press, 2002); William James, *Understanding Poststructuralism* (New York: Routledge, 2005); Martin Middeke and Timo Müller, "Poststructuralism/Deconstruction," in *English and American Studies: Theory and Practice*, ed. Martin Middeke, Timo Müller, Christina Wald, and Hubert Zapf (Stuttgart: J. B. Metzler, 2012), 197–203.

25. Jacques Derrida, *Margins of Philosophy*, trans. Alan Bass (Chicago: University of Chicago Press, 1982), 135.

26. Derrida, 135. It should also be noted that *Difference and Repetition* was the title of a book by another poststructuralist thinker, Gilles Deleuze.

27. Derrida, *Positions*, 41.

28. Derrida, 42.

29. Derrida, 41.

30. Derrida, 41.

31. Derrida, 42.

32. Derrida, 43.

33. Derrida, *Margins of Philosophy*, 329.

34. Derrida, *Positions*, 81. The question "What remains of Hegel?" redeploys and makes reference to the opening line in Derrida's *Glas*, trans. John P. Leavy and Richard Rand (Lincoln: University of Nebraska Press, 1986), a book-length engagement with the legacy of Hegelian philosophy: "What, after all, of the remain(s), today for us, here, now, of a Hegel?" This first line, which is already a challenging/difficult read, is indicative of the content and form of the rest (or the remainder) of the text, which deliberately and quite strategically strains against the very limits of readability, so much so that the book remains largely unread. As John Sturrock wrote at the end of his review of the book for the *New York Times* ("The Book Is Dead. Long Live the Book," September 13, 1987; italics in original): "*Glas* itself, I fear, asks too much of one's patience and intelligence; our defense against a text declaring itself to be unreadable may be to call its author's bluff and simply leave it unread."

35. Georg Wilhelm Friedrich Hegel, *The Phenomenology of Spirit*, trans. A. V. Miller (Oxford: Oxford University Press, 1977), 1. Translation modified.

36. Gustav E. Mueller, "The Hegel Legend of 'Thesis-Antithesis-Synthesis,'" *Journal of the History of Ideas* 19, no. 3 (1958): 411–414.

37. For those interested in the details, Mueller's analysis demonstrates how this rather wide-spread mischaracterization of Hegelian philosophy can be traced to the work of Karl Marx, who had inherited the "thesis-antithesis-synthesis" caricature from Heinrich Moritz Chalybäus, a long since forgotten expositor of the philosophy of Kant and Hegel.

38. Georg Wilhelm Friedrich Hegel, *The Science of Logic*, trans. A. V. Miller (Atlantic Highlands, NJ: Humanities Press International, 1989), 82.

39. Hegel, *The Science of Logic*, 831; italics in original.

40. Hegel, 835.

41. Hegel, 107.

42. Hegel, 105.

43. It is of course possible to modify and retool the substantive formula to take this into account by stipulating that every synthetic resolution does, in fact, pass over into a new thesis. The American philosopher and animal rights advocate, Peter Singer, for example, provides this kind of explanation in his *Hegel: A Very Short Introduction* (Oxford: Oxford University Press, 2001): "Every dialectical movement terminates with a synthesis, but not every synthesis brings the dialectical process to a stop. . . . Often the synthesis, though adequately reconciling the previous thesis and antithesis, will turn out to be

one-sided in some other respect. It will then serve as the thesis for a new dialectical movement, and so the process will continue."

44. Hegel, *The Science of Logic*, 842; italics in original.

45. Michel Foucault, *The Archaeology of Knowledge*, trans. A. M. Sheridan Smith (New York: Pantheon Books, 1972), 235.

46. This close proximity to Hegel, means that deconstruction is always running the risk of being reappropriated into Hegelian philosophy. Slavoj Žižek, in the book *For They Know Not What They Do* (London: Verso, 2008, 85), furnishes what is arguably one of the best examples, if not the definitive symptom, of this effort at reabsorption and domestication: "What the Derridean deconstruction brings out after a great struggle and declares to be the inherent limit of dialectical mediation—the point at which the movement of *Aufhebung* necessarily fails—Hegel posits directly as the crucial moment of this movement." It should also be noted that Žižek's engagement with the work of Derrida, which is given its most sustained and extended treatment in this book, is complicated by the fact that Žižek says little or nothing in response to Derrida's own writings and texts but relies heavily on their subsequent representations in Rodolphe Gasché's *The Tain of the Mirror* (Cambridge, MA: Harvard University Press, 1986).

47. This is another one of those characteristically Derridean gestures that seem to get on people's nerves. On numerous occasions, Derrida has answered pointed questions with what appears to be an ambivalent "yes and no." As diagnosed by Jeffrey Nealon, in *Double Reading: Postmodernism after Deconstruction* (Ithaca, NY: Cornell University Press, 1993, 161): "Yes and no. These are three words that are expected from a 'deconstructionist.' Whether one finds them rhetorically evasive (a sign of deconstruction's endless ethico-political waffling) or philosophically necessary (a necessarily complex rewriting of the transcendentalist 'yes or no'), these three words are, at least, a familiarly deconstructive response to a pointed question." And it is a "familiarly deconstructive response," precisely because "yes/no" constitutes another binary opposition that deconstruction would, in a word, need to deconstruct.

48. Scott Cutler Shershow, *Deconstructing Dignity: A Critique of the Right-to-Die Debate* (Chicago: University of Chicago Press, 2014), 6. In an essay that addresses the work of Bataille—"From Restricted to General Economy"—and is included in the book *Writing and Difference* (Chicago: University of Chicago Press, 1978, 267–268; italics in original), Derrida explained the difference this way: "This writing (and without concern for instruction, this is the example it provides for us, what we are interested in here, today) folds itself in order to link up with classical concepts—insofar as they are inevitable—in such a way

that these concepts, through a certain twist, apparently obey their habitual laws; but they do so while relating themselves, at a certain point, to the moment of sovereignty, to the absolute loss of their meaning, to expenditure without reserve, to what can no longer even be called negativity or loss of meaning except on its philosophical side; thus, they relate themselves to a nonmeaning which is beyond absolute meaning, beyond the closure or the horizon of absolute knowledge. Carried away in this calculated sliding, concepts become nonconcepts, they are unthinkable, they become *untenable*."

49. Jacques Derrida, *Dissemination*, trans. Barbara Johnson (Chicago: University of Chicago Press, 1981), 6.

50. Derrida, *Positions*, 42.

Chapter 4

1. Michael Naas, *Miracle and Machine: Jacques Derrida and the Two Sources of Religion, Science, and the Media* (New York: Fordham University Press, 2012), 8. For those of us armed with digital technology, mobile devices, and cloud-based data services, the deconstruction of logocentrism, though important and influential, could be easily dismissed for "not speaking to us" and therefore relegated to a moment in late twentieth-century literary studies. If deconstruction is to be more than a legacy system, seen receding behind us in the rear-view mirror of history, we need to make it able to respond to (and responsible for) the opportunities and challenges of the present and not-too-distant future. It needs to be uploaded to the twenty first century.

2. Aristotle, *Aristotle I: Categories. On Interpretation. Prior Analytics*, trans. H. P. Cooke (Cambridge, MA: Harvard University Press, 1938), 16a, 3.

3. The word "logocentrism" predates Derrida. As reported by Michael Harrison in the term posting on the *Chicago School of Media Theory* website, https://lucian.uchicago.edu/blogs/mediatheory/keywords/logocentrism/: "It first appeared in academic writing around 1929 as the German *Logozentrisch* in the work of philosopher and psychologist Ludwig Klages. *The Oxford English Dictionary*, which defines 'logocentric' as, simply, 'centered on reason,' claims the word was first used in English by theologian V. A. Demant in 1942 and *Dictionnaire Le Robert* cites its first use in French in 1942."

4. Jacques Derrida, *Of Grammatology*, trans. Gayatri Chakravorty Spivak (Baltimore: Johns Hopkins University Press, 1976), 11.

5. Plato, *Plato I: Euthyphro, Apology, Crito, Phaedo, Phaedrus*, trans. H. N. Fowler (Cambridge, MA: Harvard University Press, 1982), 228e.

6. Walter Ong, *Orality and Literacy: The Technologizing of the Word* (New York: Routledge, 1995), 81–82.

7. This is so "natural" that we barely notice that the privilege of speech is only able to be established and justified in and by writing. It is this apparent contradiction—what Derrida calls the "written proposal of logocentrism" in *Dissemination*, trans. Barbara Johnson (Chicago: University of Chicago Press, 1981, 158)—that provides the occasion and justification for its deconstruction.

8. For this reason, many subsequent forms of media and communication technology have been identified with names that literally connect them to writing, i.e., photography ("light writing"), cinematography ("movement writing"), telegraphy ("distant writing"), or phonography ("sound writing").

9. Plato, *Plato I*, 275d–276a.

10. Plato, 276a.

11. Derrida, *Dissemination*, 91–92. This also explains why, in music in particular, the original performance of a song or a piece of music is called "live" and distinguished from recorded reproductions, or what are called "records." For a detailed examination and deconstruction of this entire axiological system, see David J. Gunkel's *Of Remixology: Ethics and Aesthetics after Remix* (Cambridge, MA: MIT Press, 2016).

12. Gunkel, *Of Remixology*, 103.

13. Gunkel, 103.

14. René Wellek, "Destroying Literary Studies," *New Criterion* 2, no. 4 (December 1983): 3, https://newcriterion.com/issues/1983/12/destroying-literary -studies.

15. Jacques Derrida, *Memoires for Paul de Man*, trans. Cecile Lindsay, Jonathan Culler, and Eduardo Cadava (New York: Columbia University Press, 1986), 42.

16. Jacques Derrida, "Signature Event Context," trans. Samuel Weber and Jeffrey Mehlman, in *Limited Inc*, ed. Gerald Graff (Evanston, IL: Northwestern University Press, 1993), 21; italics in original.

17. Derrida, *Of Grammatology*, 323.

18. Derrida, "Signature Event Context," 20.

19. Plato, *Phaedrus*, 275d–e.

20. Plato, 276a.

21. Jacques Derrida, *Positions*, trans. Alan Bass (Chicago: University of Chicago Press), 82.

22. Plato, *Plato VI: Republic II*, trans. Paul Shorey (Cambridge, MA: Harvard University Press, 1987), 515a–b.

23. Plato, *Plato VI*, 515a–b.

24. It is this repetition that is called out and identified by that famous statement from Alfred North Whitehead in *Process and Reality: An Essay in*

Cosmology (New York: The Free Press, 1985: 39): "The safest general characterization of the European philosophical tradition is that it consists of a series of footnotes to Plato."

25. Robert Nozick, *Anarchy, State, and Utopia* (New York: Basic Books, 1974), 42.

26. Nozick, *Anarchy, State, and Utopia*, 44.

27. The pharmacological metaphor that organizes the narrative trajectory of *The Matrix*—the either/or choice between two different pills—is something that is not original to the film. In fact, it is already apparent and operationalized in Plato's *Phaedrus*. In the legend of Theuth and Thamus that concludes the dialogue, writing is associated with drugs and positioned as either a medicine that will lead to enhanced cognitive capabilities or a narcotic that will degrade and poison the mind with deceptions. This is why Derrida's essay on the *Phaedrus* is titled "Plato's Pharmacy." For more on this subject, see "VRx: Media Technology, Drugs, and Codependency" in David J. Gunkel, *Thinking Otherwise: Philosophy, Communication, Technology* (West Lafayette, IN: Purdue University Press, 2007).

28. Sherry Turkle, *Alone Together: Why We Expect More from Technology and Less from Each Other* (New York: Basic Books, 2011).

29. Friedrich Nietzsche, *Nachgelassene Fragmente 1869–1874*, in *Friedrich Nietzsche Sämtliche Werke Kritische Studienausgabe*, vol. 7, ed. Giorgio Colli and Mazzino Montinari (Berlin: Walter de Gruyter, 1980), 199. Translation by the author.

30. Friedrich Nietzsche, *Twilight of the Idols*, in *The Portable Nietzsche*, ed. and trans. Walter Kaufmann (New York: Penguin Books, 1983), 485; italics in original.

31. Pierre Lévy, *Cyberculture*, trans. Robert Bononno (Minneapolis: University of Minnesota Press, 2001), 29.

32. Slavoj Žižek, *Organs without Bodies: On Deleuze and Consequences* (New York: Routledge, 2004), 3.

33. Gilles Deleuze, *Difference and Repetition*, trans. Paul Patton (New York: Columbia University Press, 1994), 209. The points of contact and contrast between Deleuze and Derrida are complex and worth an investigative effort in their own right. For more on this subject, see Paul Patton and John Protevi, *Between Deleuze and Derrida* (New York: Continuum, 2003).

34. Deleuze, *Difference and Repetition*, 211.

35. Derek Stanovsky, "Virtual Reality," in *The Blackwell Guide to the Philosophy of Computing and Information*, ed. Luciano Florid (Oxford: Blackwell Publishing, 2004), 171.

36. William Gibson, "God's Little Toys: Confessions of a Cut and Paste Artist," *Wired* 13, no. 7 (July 2005): 119, https://www.wired.com/2005/07/gibson-3/; Kirby Ferguson, *Everything Is a Remix* (film) (2015), https://www.everythingisaremix.info/watch-the-series.

37. Brett Gaylor, *Rip!: A Remix Manifesto* (Montreal: Eye Steel Film, 2008), http://ripremix.com/.

38. Benjamin Franzen and Kembrew McLeod, *Copyright Criminals*, aired January 18, 2010, on PBS documentary series *Independent Lens*, http://www.copyrightcriminals.com/.

39. Henry Rollins, "Henry Rollins on Rave and Modern Rock Music," *YouTube*, 2007, https://www.youtube.com/watch?v=AyRDDOpKaLM.

40. Andrew Whelan and Katharina Freund, "Remix: Practice, Context, Culture," *M/C Journal* 16, no. 4 (2013), http://journal.media-culture.org.au/index.php/mcjournal/article/view/694.

41. Gilles Deleuze, *Negotiations*, trans. Martin Joughin (New York: Columbia University Press, 1995), 67.

42. Donna J. Haraway, *Simians, Cyborgs, and Women: The Reinvention of Nature* (New York: Routledge, 1991), 177.

43. Haraway, *Simians, Cyborgs, and Women*, 181.

44. Manfred E. Clynes and Nathan S. Kline, "Cyborgs and Space," in *The Cyborg Handbook*, ed. Chris Hables Gray (New York: Routledge, 1995), 29.

45. Clynes and Kline, "Cyborgs and Space," 30–31.

46. Haraway, *Simians, Cyborgs, and Women*, 174.

47. Haraway, 150.

48. Haraway, 151–152.

49. Joanna Zylinska, *Bioethics in the Age of New Media* (Cambridge, MA: MIT Press, 2009), 12.

50. Haraway, *Simians, Cyborgs, and Women*, 173.

51. N. Katherine Hayles, *How We Became Posthuman: Virtual Bodies in Cybernetics, Literature and Informatics* (Chicago: University of Chicago Press, 1999), 286.

Chapter 5

1. Jacques Derrida, "Afterword," trans. Samuel Weber, in *Limited Inc*, ed. Gerald Graff (Evanston, IL: Northwestern University Press, 1993), 116–117.

2. Friedrich Nietzsche, *Thus Spoke Zarathustra,* in *The Portable Nietzsche*, ed. and trans. Walter Kaufmann (New York: Penguin Books, 1983), 146.

3. William Gibson, *Neuromancer* (New York: Ace Books, 1984).

4. Ray Kurzweil, *The Singularity Is Near: When Humans Transcend Biology* (New York: Viking, 2005). Nick Bostrom, *Superintelligence: Paths, Dangers, Strategies* (New York: Oxford University Press, 2014).

5. Jacques Derrida, *Who's Afraid of Philosophy: Right to Philosophy 1*, trans. Jan Plug (Stanford, CA: Stanford University Press, 2002), 103.

6. Jacques Derrida, "Limited Inc a b c . . . ," trans. Samuel Weber, in *Limited Inc*, ed. Gerald Graff (Evanston, IL: Northwestern University Press, 1993), 90. Gayatri Chakravorty Spivak, "Gayatri Spivak on Derrida, the Subaltern, and Her Life and Work," *E-flux conversations* (August 1, 2016), https://conversations.e-flux.com/t/gayatri-spivak-on-derrida-the-subaltern-and-her-life-and-work/4198; Donna J. Haraway, "A Cyborg Manifesto: Science, Technology, and Socialist-Feminism in the Late Twentieth Century," in *Simians, Cyborgs, and Women: The Reinvention of Nature* (New York: Routledge, 1991), 149.

7. Haraway, "A Cyborg Manifesto," 150; italics in original.

8. Gloria Anzaldúa, *Borderlands/La Frontera* (San Francisco, CA: Spinsters/Aunt Lute, 1987). Trinh T. Minh-ha, *Woman Native Other: Writing Postcoloniality and Feminism* (Bloomington: Indiana University Press, 1989).

9. Constance Penley and Andrew Ross, "Cyborgs at Large: Interview with Donna Haraway," in *Technoculture*, ed. Constance Penley and Andrew Ross (Minneapolis: University of Minnesota Press, 1991), 12.

10. Penley and Ross, "Cyborgs at Large," 12–13.

11. Mark Taylor, "What Derrida Really Meant," *New York Times*, October 14, 2004, https://www.nytimes.com/2004/10/14/opinion/what-derrida-really-meant.html.

12. Derrida, "Afterword," 148.

13. Derrida, 148.

14. Plato, *Plato I: Euthyphro, Apology, Crito, Phaedo, Phaedrus*, trans. H. N. Fowler (Cambridge, MA: Harvard University Press, 1982), 96a. This reading/interpretation of the *Phaedo* is indebted to and informed by the work of John Sallis, especially the book *Spacings—Of Reason, and Imagination* (Chicago: University of Chicago Press, 1987).

15. Plato, *Plato I*, 99e.

16. Plato, 100a.

17. Briankle Chang, *Deconstructing Communication: Representation, Subject, and Economies of Exchange* (Minneapolis: University of Minnesota Press, 1996), x.

18. Jacques Derrida, *Positions*, trans. Alan Bass (Chicago: University of Chicago Press, 1981), 44.

19. Derrida, 41.

20. Derrida, 71.

21. Derrida, "Afterword," 147.

22. Jacques Derrida, *Dissemination*, trans. Barbara Johnson (Chicago: University of Chicago Press, 1981), 5.

23. Derrida, *Positions*, 42; italics in original.

24. Derrida, 42.

25. Derrida, 42.

26. Mark Taylor, *Hiding* (Chicago: University of Chicago Press, 1997), 325.

27. Taylor, *Hiding*, 270.

28. Plato, *Plato VII: Theaetetus, Sophist*, trans. H. N. Fowler (Cambridge, MA: Harvard University Press, 1987), 174a.

29. As explained in chapter 1, this is one of the main reasons why deconstruction cannot be construed and operationalized as a method in the usual sense of the word.

30. Georg Wilhelm Friedrich Hegel, *Enzyklopädie der philosophischen Wissenschaften im Grundrisse* (Hamburg: Verlag von Felix Meiner, 1969), 137. Translation by the author. Although Hegel was no computer scientist, his concept of the "bad or spurious infinite" is remarkably similar to recursion, a fundamental aspect of computational operations that defines an infinite number of instances by using a set of finite expressions.

31. Plato, *Plato I*, 23a.

32. Not for nothing, but the division of the discipline of philosophy into analytic vs. continental is one more binary opposition that is/should be the subject of (or subjected to) deconstruction.

33. Daniel Dennett, *Kinds of Minds* (New York: Basic Books, 1996), vii.

34. Slavoj Žižek, "Philosophy, the 'Unknown Knowns,' and the Public Use of Reason," *Topoi* 25, no. 1–2 (September 2006): 137, https://doi.org/10.1007/s11245-006-0021-2.

BIBLIOGRAPHY

Allen, Woody. *Deconstructing Harry*. New York: Fine Line Features, 1998.

Anzaldúa, Gloria. *Borderlands/La Frontera*. San Francisco, CA: Spinsters/Aunt Lute, 1987.

Arac, Jonathan, Wlad Godzich, and Wallace Martin. *The Yale Critics: Deconstruction in America*. Minneapolis: University of Minnesota Press, 1986.

Arendt, Hannah. *Thinking without a Banister: Essays in Understanding 1953–1975*. New York: Schocken Books, 2018.

Aristotle. *Aristotle I: Categories. On Interpretation. Prior Analytics*, translated by H. P. Cooke. Cambridge, MA: Harvard University Press, 1938.

Aristotle. *Aristotle XVII: The Metaphysics, Bk. I–IX*, translated by Hugh Tredennick. Cambridge, MA: Harvard University Press, 1980.

Artise, Bridgett, and Jen Karetnick. *Born-Again Vintage: 25 Ways to Deconstruct, Reinvent, and Recycle Your Wardrobe*. New York: Potter Craft, 2008.

Barthes, Roland. "Death of the Author." In *Image, Music, Text*, translated by Stephen Heath, 142–148. New York: Hill & Wang, 1978.

Baudrillard, Jean. *The Intelligence of Evil, or the Lucidity Pact*, translated by Chris Turner. Oxford: Berg, 2005.

Belsey, Catherine. *Poststructuralism: A Very Short Introduction*. New York: Oxford University Press, 2002.

Bloom, Harold, Paul De Man, Jacques Derrida, Geoffrey H. Hartman, and J. Hillis Miller. *Deconstruction and Criticism*, edited by Geoffrey H. Hartman. New York: Continuum, 1979.

Bolter, Jay David. *Writing Space: The Computer, Hypertext, and the History of Writing*. Hillsdale, NJ: Lawrence Erlbaum Associates, 1991.

Bostrom, Nick. *Superintelligence: Paths, Dangers, Strategies*. New York: Oxford University Press, 2014.

Buchanan, Ian. *A Dictionary of Critical Theory*. New York: Oxford University Press, 2016.

Burman, Erica. *Deconstructing Developmental Psychology*. New York: Routledge, 2016.

Campbell, Colin. "The Tyranny of the Yale Critics." *New York Times Magazine*, February 9, 1986. https://www.nytimes.com/1986/02/09/magazine/the-tyranny -of-the-yale-critics.html.

Caputo, John D. *Deconstruction in a Nutshell: A Conversation with Jacques Derrida*. New York: Fordham University Press, 1997.

Chandler, Daniel. *Semiotics: The Basics*. New York: Routledge, 2002.

Chang, Briankle. *Deconstructing Communication: Representation, Subject, and Economies of Exchange*. Minneapolis: University of Minnesota Press, 1996.

Clynes, Manfred E., and Nathan S. Kline. "Cyborgs and Space." In *The Cyborg Handbook*, edited by Chris Hables Gray, 29–33. New York: Routledge, 1995.

Creech, James, Peggy Kamuf, and Jane Todd. "Deconstruction in America: An Interview with Jacques Derrida." *Critical Exchange* 17 (Winter 1985): 1–32.

Critchley, Simon. *The Ethics of Deconstruction*. Edinburgh: Edinburgh University Press, 2014

Culler, Jonathan. *On Deconstruction: Theory and Criticism after Structuralism*. Ithaca, NY: Cornell University Press, 1992.

Currie, Mark. *The Invention of Deconstruction*. New York: Palgrave Macmillan, 2013.

Deleuze, Gilles. *Difference and Repetition*, translated by P. Patton. New York: Columbia University Press, 1994.

Deleuze, Gilles. *Negotiations*, translated by Martin Joughin. New York: Columbia University Press, 1995.

De Man, Paul. *Allegories of Reading: Figural Language in Rousseau, Nietzsche, Rilke and Proust*. New Haven, CT: Yale University Press, 1979.

Dennett, Daniel. *Kinds of Minds*. New York: Basic Books, 1996.

Derrida, Jacques. *Dissemination*, translated by Barbara Johnson. Chicago: University of Chicago Press, 1981.

Derrida, Jacques. *Glas*, translated by John P. Leavy and Richard Rand. Lincoln: University of Nebraska Press, 1986.

Derrida, Jacques. *Limited Inc*, edited by Gerald Graff, translated by Samuel Weber and Jeffrey Mehlman. Evanston, IL: Northwestern University Press, 1993.

Derrida, Jacques. *Margins of Philosophy*, translated by Alan Bass. Chicago: University of Chicago Press, 1982.

Derrida, Jacques. *Memoires for Paul de Man*, translated by Cecile Lindsay, Jonathan Culler, and Eduardo Cadava. New York: Columbia University Press, 1986.

Derrida, Jacques. *Negotiations: Interventions and Interviews, 1971–2001*, edited and translated by Elizabeth G. Rottenberg. Stanford, CA: Stanford University Press, 2002.

Derrida, Jacques. *Of Grammatology*, translated by Gayatri Chakravorty Spivak. Baltimore: Johns Hopkins University Press, 1976.

Derrida, Jacques. *Points . . . Interviews, 1974–1994*, edited by Elisabeth Weber. Stanford, CA: Stanford University Press, 1995.

Derrida, Jacques. *Positions*, translated by Alan Bass. Chicago: University of Chicago Press, 1981.

Derrida, Jacques. *Psyche: Inventions of the Other*, vol. 1, edited by Peggy Kamuf and Elizabeth G. Rottenberg. Stanford, CA: Stanford University Press, 2007.

Derrida, Jacques. *Psyche: Inventions of the Other*, vol. 2, edited by Peggy Kamuf and Elizabeth G. Rottenberg. Stanford, CA: Stanford University Press, 2008.

Derrida, Jacques. *Who's Afraid of Philosophy: Right to Philosophy 1*, trans. Jan Plug. Stanford, CA: Stanford University Press, 2002.

Derrida, Jacques. *Writing and Difference*, translated by Alan Bass. Chicago: University of Chicago Press, 1978.

Donoghue, Denis. "Deconstructing Deconstruction." *New York Review of Books*, June 12, 1980. https://www.nybooks.com/articles/1980/06/12/deconstructing-deconstruction/.

Elbow, Peter. "The Uses of Binary Thinking." *Journal of Advanced Composition* 13, no. 1 (1993): 51–78. http://www.jaconlinejournal.com/archives/vol13.1/elbow-uses.pdf.

Ettlinger, Steve. *Twinkie, Deconstructed: My Journey to Discover How the Ingredients Found in Processed Foods Are Grown, Mined (Yes, Mined), and Manipulated into What America Eats*. New York: Hudson Street Press, 2008.

Ferguson, Kirby. *Everything Is a Remix—Remastered* (film), 2015. https://www
.everythingisaremix.info/watch-the-series.

Foucault, Michel. *The Archaeology of Knowledge*, translated by A. M. Sheridan
Smith. New York: Pantheon Books, 1972.

Foucault, Michel. "What Is an Author?," translated by Josué V. Harari. In *The
Foucault Reader*, edited by Paul Rabinow, 101–120. New York: Pantheon Books,
1984.

Franzen, Benjamin, and Kembrew McLeod. *Copyright Criminals*. Aired January 18, 2010, on PBS documentary series *Independent Lens*, http://www
.copyrightcriminals.com/.

Freiman, Scott. *Deconstructing the Beatles*, 2020. http://www.beatleslectures
.com/.

Gasché, Rodolphe. *The Tain of the Mirror: Derrida and the Philosophy of Reflection*.
Cambridge, MA: Harvard University Press, 1987.

Gaylor, Brett. *Rip!: A Remix Manifesto*. Montreal: Eye Steel Film, 2008. http://
ripremix.com/.

Gibson, William. "God's Little Toys: Confessions of a Cut and Paste Artist." *Wired* 13, no. 7 (July 2005): 118–119. https://www.wired.com/2005/07
/gibson-3/.

Gibson, William. *Neuromancer*. New York: Ace Books, 1984.

Gill, Alison. "Deconstruction Fashion: The Making of Unfinished, Decomposing and Re-assembled Clothes." *Fashion Theory* 2, no. 1 (1998): 25–49. https://
doi.org/10.2752/136270498779754489.

Godzich, Wlad. "The Domestication of Derrida." In *The Yale Critics: Deconstruction in America*, edited by Jonathan Arac, Wlad Godzich, and Wallace Martin,
20–42. Minneapolis: University of Minnesota Press, 1986.

Goldblatt, Mark. "*Derrida*, Derrida, Etc." *National Review*, January 16, 2003.
https://www.nationalreview.com/2003/01/derrida-derrida-etc-mark-goldblatt/.

Gottlieb, Paula. "Aristotle on Non-contradiction." *Stanford Encyclopedia of Philosophy*, 2019. https://plato.stanford.edu/entries/aristotle-noncontradiction/.

Greene, Brian. *The Fabric of the Cosmos: Space, Time, and the Texture of Reality*.
New York: Vintage Books, 2005.

Gunkel, David J. *Hacking Cyberspace*. New York: Routledge, 2001.

Gunkel, David J. *Of Remixology: Ethics and Aesthetics after Remix*. Cambridge, MA: MIT Press, 2016.

Gunkel, David J. "VRx: Media Technology, Drugs, and Codependency." In *Thinking Otherwise: Philosophy, Communication, Technology*, 82–102. West Lafayette, IN: Purdue University Press, 2007.

Haraway, Donna J. *Simians, Cyborgs, and Women: The Reinvention of Nature*. New York: Routledge, 1991.

Hayles, N. Katherine. *How We Became Posthuman: Virtual Bodies in Cybernetics, Literature and Informatics*. Chicago: University of Chicago Press, 1999.

Hegel, Georg Wilhelm Friedrich. *Enzyklopädie der philosophischen Wissenschaften im Grundrisse*. Hamburg: Verlag von Felix Meiner, 1969.

Hegel, Georg Wilhelm Friedrich. *The Phenomenology of Spirit*, translated by A. V. Miller. Oxford: Oxford University Press, 1977.

Hegel, Georg Wilhelm Friedrich. *The Science of Logic*, translated by A. V. Miller. Atlantic Highlands, NJ: Humanities Press International, 1989.

Heidegger, Martin. *Being and Time*, translated by John Macquarrie and Edward Robinson. New York: Harper & Row, 1962.

Hellerman, Jason. "Deconstructing Film Lighting: What Kinds of Sources Do the Pros Use?" *No Film School*, 2019. https://nofilmschool.com/Deconstructing-film-lighting.

Hogue, W. Lawrence. "Radical Democracy, African American (Male) Subjectivity, and John Edgar Wideman's *Philadelphia Fire*." *Melus* 33, no. 3 (September 1, 2008): 45–69. https://doi.org/10.1093/melus/33.3.45.

James, William. *Understanding Poststructuralism*. New York: Routledge, 2005.

Johnson, Barbara. *A World of Difference*. Baltimore: Johns Hopkins University Press, 1987.

Kandell, Jonathan. "Jacques Derrida, Abstruse Theorist, Dies at 74." *New York Times*, October 10, 2004. https://www.nytimes.com/2004/10/10/obituaries/jacques-derrida-abstruse-theorist-dies-at-74.html.

Kurzweil, Ray. *The Singularity Is Near: When Humans Transcend Biology*. New York: Viking, 2005.

Lean, Lucy. *Made in America: Our Best Chefs Reinvent Comfort Food*. New York: Welcome Books, 2011.

Leitch, Vincent B. *Literary Criticism in the 21st Century: Theory Renaissance*. New York: Bloomsbury, 2014.

Lévy, Pierre. *Cyberculture*, translated by Robert Bononno. Minneapolis: University of Minnesota Press, 2001.

London Film School. "Deconstructing the Soundtrack: A School of Sound Masterclass," 2020. https://lfs.org.uk/workshops/lfs-workshops/252/deconstructing-soundtrack-school-sound-seminar-series.

Lorde, Audre. *Sister Outsider: Essays and Speeches*. Berkeley, CA: The Crossing Press, 1984.

Macaulay, Alastair. "The Many Faces of 'Black Swan,' Deconstructed." *New York Times*, February 9, 2011. https://www.nytimes.com/2011/02/10/arts/dance/10swan.html.

Meyich, Elissa. *Rip It! How to Deconstruct and Reconstruct the Clothes of Your Dreams*. New York: Simon & Schuster, 2006.

Middeke, Martin, and Timo Müller. "Poststructuralism/Deconstruction." In *English and American Studies: Theory and Practice*, edited by Martin Middeke, Timo Müller, Christina Wald, and Hubert Zapf, 197–203. Stuttgart: J. B. Metzler, 2012. https://doi.org/10.1007/978-3-476-00406-2_8.

Miller, J. Hillis. *For Derrida*. New York: Fordham University Press, 2009.

Mueller, Gustav E. "The Hegel Legend of 'Thesis-Antithesis-Synthesis.'" *Journal of the History of Ideas* 19, no. 3 (1958): 411–414. https://www.jstor.org/stable/2708045.

Naas, Michael. *Miracle and Machine: Jacques Derrida and the Two Sources of Religion, Science, and the Media*. New York: Fordham University Press, 2012.

Nealon, Jeffrey T. *Double Reading: Postmodernism after Deconstruction*. Ithaca, NY: Cornell University Press, 1993.

Nietzsche, Friedrich. *Beyond Good and Evil*, translated by Walter Kaufmann. New York: Vintage Books, 1989.

Nietzsche, Friedrich. *Nachgelassene Fragmente 1869–1874*. In *Friedrich Nietzsche Sämtliche Werke Kritische Studienausgabe*, vol. 7, edited by Giorgio Colli and Mazzino Montinari. Berlin: Walter de Gruyter, 1980.

Nietzsche, Friedrich. *Thus Spoke Zarathustra*. In *The Portable Nietzsche*, edited and translated by Walter Kaufmann. New York: Penguin Books, 1983.

Nietzsche, Friedrich. *Twilight of the Idols*. In *The Portable Nietzsche*, edited and translated by Walter Kaufmann, 463–563. New York: Penguin Books, 1983.

Nozick, Robert. *Anarchy, State, and Utopia*. New York: Basic Books, 1974.

Ong, Walter. *Orality and Literacy: The Technologizing of the Word*. New York: Routledge, 1995.

Orlet, Christopher. "Derrida's Bluff." *The American Spectator*, October 15, 2004. https://spectator.org/49462_derridas-bluff/.

Patton, Paul, and John Protevi. *Between Deleuze and Derrida*. New York: Continuum, 2003.

Penley, Constance, and Andrew Ross. "Cyborgs at Large: Interview with Donna Haraway." In *Technoculture*, edited by Constance Penley and Andrew Ross, 1–26. Minneapolis: University of Minnesota Press, 1991.

Plato. *Plato I: Euthyphro, Apology, Crito, Phaedo, Phaedrus*, translated by H. N. Fowler. Cambridge, MA: Harvard University Press, 1982.

Plato. *Plato VI: Republic II*, translated by P. Shorey. Cambridge, MA: Harvard University Press, 1987.

Plato. *Plato VII: Theaetetus, Sophist*, translated by H. N. Fowler. Cambridge, MA: Harvard University Press, 1987.

Putnam, Hillary. *Renewing Philosophy*. Cambridge, MA: Harvard University Press, 1992.

Rahman, Mohammad. *C# Deconstructed: Discover How C# Works on the .NET Framework*. New York: Apress, 2014.

Redfield, Marc. *Theory at Yale: The Strange Case of Deconstruction in America*. New York: Fordham University Press, 2016.

Roberts, Jennifer. *Redux: Designs That Reuse, Recycle, and Reveal*. Salt Lake City: Gibbs Smith. 2005.

Rolfe, Gary. "Deconstruction in a Nutshell." *Nursing Philosophy* 5, no. 3 (2004): 274–276. https://doi.org/10.1111/j.1466-769X.2004.00179.x.

Rollins, Henry. 2007. "Henry Rollins on Rave and Modern Rock Music." You-Tube. https://www.youtube.com/watch?v=AyRDDOpKaLM.

Saint Augustine. *Confessions*, translated by R. S. Pine-Coffin. New York: Penguin Classics, 1981.

Sallis, John. *Spacings—Of Reason, and Imagination*. Chicago: University of Chicago Press, 1987.

Saussure, Ferdinand de. *Course in General Linguistics*, translated by Wade Baskin. London: Peter Owen, 1959.

Scott, A. O. "Deconstructing the Realities of Politics and Terrorism." *New York Times*, December 9, 2005. https://www.nytimes.com/2005/12/09/movies/deconstructing-the-realities-of-politics-and-terrorism.html.

Shershow, Scott Cutler. *Deconstructing Dignity: A Critique of the Right-to-Die Debate*. Chicago: University of Chicago Press, 2014.

Singer, Peter. *Hegel: A Very Short Introduction*. Oxford: Oxford University Press, 2001.

Smith, Barry, Hans Albert, David Armstrong, Ruth Barcan Marcus, Keith Campbell, Richard Glauser, Rudolf Haller, Massimo Mugnai, Kevin Mulligan, Lorenzo Peña, Willard van Orman Quine, Wolfgang Röd, Edmund Ruggaldier, Karl Schuhmann, Daniel Schulthess, Peter Simons, René Thom, Dallas Willard, and Jan Wolenski. "Open letter against Derrida receiving an honorary doctorate from Cambridge University," *Times*, May 9, 1992. Reprinted in *Cambridge Review* 113 (October 1992): 138–139, and in Jacques Derrida, *Points . . . Interviews, 1974–1994*, edited by Elisabeth Weber, 419–421. Stanford, CA: Stanford University Press, 1995.

Spivak, Gayatri Chakravorty. "Gayatri Spivak on Derrida, the Subaltern, and Her Life and Work." *E-flux conversations*, August 1, 2016. https://conversations.e-flux.com/t/gayatri-spivak-on-derrida-the-subaltern-and-her-life-and-work/4198.

Spivak, Gayatri Chakravorty. *In Other Worlds: Essays in Cultural Politics*. New York: Routledge, 1998.

Stables, Andrew. "Deconstructing Deconstruction." *English in Education* 26, no. 3 (1992): 19–23. https://doi.org/10.1111/j.1754-8845.1992.tb01076.x.

Stanovsky, Derek. "Virtual Reality." In *The Blackwell Guide to the Philosophy of Computing and Information*, edited by Luciano Floridi, 167–177. Oxford: Blackwell Publishing, 2004.

St. Fleur, Nicholas. "A Paleontologist Deconstructs 'Jurassic World.'" *New York Times*, June 12, 2015. https://www.nytimes.com/interactive/2015/06/12/science/jurassic-world-deconstructed-by-paleontologist.html.

Stich, Stephen P. *Deconstructing the Mind*. Oxford: Oxford University Press, 1998.

Sturrock, John. "The Book Is Dead. Long Live the Book." *New York Times*, September 13, 1987. https://www.nytimes.com/1987/09/13/books/the-book-is-dead-long-live-the-book.html.

Suchocki, Marjorie Hewitt. "Deconstructing Deconstruction: Language, Process, and a Theology of Nature." *American Journal of Theology & Philosophy* 11, no. 2 (1990): 133–142. https://www.jstor.org/stable/27943772.

Taylor, Mark C. *Hiding*. Chicago: University of Chicago Press, 1997.

Taylor, Mark. C. "What Derrida Really Meant." *New York Times*, October 14, 2004. https://www.nytimes.com/2004/10/14/opinion/what-derrida-really-meant.html.

Thomas, Gary, and Andrew Loxley. *Deconstructing Special Education and Constructing Inclusion*. New York: Open University Press, 2017.

Trinh, Minh-ha T. *Woman Native Other: Writing Postcoloniality and Feminism*. Bloomington: Indiana University Press, 1989.

Turkle, Sherry. *Alone Together: Why We Expect More from Technology and Less from Each Other*. New York: Basic Books, 2011.

Wawrytko, Sandra A. "Deconstructing Deconstruction: Zhuang Zi as Butterfly, Nietzsche as Gadfly." *Philosophy East and West* 58, no. 4 (October 2008): 524–551. http://www.jstor.org/stable/40213537.

Wellek, René. "Destroying Literary Studies." *New Criterion* 2, no. 4 (December 1983): 1–7. https://newcriterion.com/issues/1983/12/destroying-literary-studies.

Whelan, Andrew, and Katharina Freund. "Remix: Practice, Context, Culture." *M/C Journal* 16, no. 4 (August 2013). http://journal.media-culture.org.au/index.php/mcjournal/article/view/694.

Whitehead, Alfred North. *Process and Reality: An Essay in Cosmology*. New York: The Free Press, 1985.

Wigley, Mark, and Philip Johnson. *Deconstructivist Architecture*. New York: Museum of Modern Art, 1998.

Žižek, Slavoj. *For They Know Not What They Do: Enjoyment as a Political Factor*. London: Verso, 2008.

Žižek, Slavoj. *Organs without Bodies: On Deleuze and Consequences*. New York: Routledge, 2004.

Žižek, Slavoj. "Philosophy, the 'Unknown Knowns,' and the Public Use of Reason," *Topoi* 25, no. 1–2 (September 2006): 137–142. https://doi.org/10.1007/s11245-006-0021-2.

Zylinska, Joanna. *Bioethics in the Age of New Media*. Cambridge, MA: MIT Press, 2009.

FURTHER READING

Bloom, Harold, Paul De Man, Jacques Derrida, Geoffrey H. Hartman, J. Hillis Miller. *Deconstruction and Criticism*, edited by Geoffrey H. Hartman. New York: Continuum, 1979.

Chang, Briankle. *Deconstructing Communication: Representation, Subject, and Economies of Exchange*. Minneapolis: University of Minnesota Press, 1996.

Culler, Jonathan. *On Deconstruction: Theory and Criticism after Structuralism*. Ithaca, NY: Cornell University Press, 1992.

Derrida, Jacques. *Dissemination*, translated by Barbara Johnson. Chicago: University of Chicago Press, 1981.

Derrida, Jacques. *Limited Inc*, edited by Gerald Graff, translated by Samuel Weber and Jeffrey Mehlman. Evanston, IL: Northwestern University Press, 1993.

Derrida, Jacques. *Of Grammatology*, translated by Gayatri Chakravorty Spivak. Baltimore: Johns Hopkins University Press, 1976.

Derrida, Jacques. *Positions*, translated by Alan Bass. Chicago: University of Chicago Press, 1981.

Derrida, Jacques. *Psyche: Inventions of the Other*, vol. 2, edited by Peggy Kamuf and Elizabeth G. Rottenberg. Stanford, CA: Stanford University Press, 2008.

Haraway, Donna J. *Simians, Cyborgs, and Women: The Reinvention of Nature*. New York: Routledge, 1991.

Johnson, Barbara. *A World of Difference*. Baltimore: Johns Hopkins University Press, 1987.

Nealon, Jeffrey T. *Double Reading: Postmodernism after Deconstruction*. Ithaca, NY: Cornell University Press, 1993.

Plato. *Plato I: Euthyphro, Apology, Crito, Phaedo, Phaedrus*, translated by H. N. Fowler. Cambridge, MA: Harvard University Press, 1982.

Plato. *Plato VI: Republic II*, translated by P. Shorey. Cambridge, MA: Harvard University Press, 1987.

Saussure, Ferdinand de. *Course in General Linguistics*, translated by Wade Baskin. London: Peter Owen, 1959.

Spivak, Gayatri Chakravorty. *In Other Worlds: Essays In Cultural Politics*. New York: Routledge, 1998.

INDEX

The MIT Press Essential Knowledge Series

DAVID J. GUNKEL is an award-winning educator, scholar, and author, specializing in the philosophy and ethics of emerging technology. He is the author of over eighty scholarly articles and book chapters and has published thirteen internationally recognized books. He currently holds the position of Distinguished Teaching Professor in the Department of Communication at Northern Illinois University. More info at http://gunkelweb.com.